RED BUD WOMEN

FOUR DRAMATIC EPISODES

By
MARK O'DEA

With a foreword by
PIERRE LOVING

One-Act Play Reprint Series

Core Collection Books, inc.

GREAT NECK, NEW YORK

First Published 1922
Reprinted 1976

International Standard Book Number
0-8486-2006-2

Library of Congress Catalog Number
76-40391

PRINTED IN THE UNITED STATES OF AMERICA

TO
THEODORE BALLOU HINCKLEY

CONTENTS

	Page
FOREWORD	vii
THE SONG OF SOLOMON	1
SHIVAREE	27
MISS MYRTLE SAYS "YES"	53
NOT IN THE LESSONS	89

FOREWORD

Some months ago in the course of a half-lounging trip, partly on foot, through the states of Kansas, Missouri and Arkansas, I came rather abruptly (with a sharp awareness!) upon that incarnate ghost which occasionally, but only occasionally, haunts the mind of the cynical analyst of our national organism. I refer, of course, to the American peasant. Previous to this, I must confess, I had to a very large extent viewed the rural population of the United States, like so many other hit-or-miss generalizers, from the narrow, remote rookeries of the cities. Thus, for me, it fell away neatly and compactly into the quite prehensible categories of farmer, miner, road-mender, and migratory harvest hand. Unhurried contact, however, with members of the widely scattered farming peoples of these and other states, with enough leisure to weigh what was heard, felt, and seen, brought home to me vividly, in no equivocal fashion, that an American peasantry of a sort—vastly diverse, to be sure, from any other kind in the world—actually exists and toils among us. When I say that our rural classes distinctly part ways with all others, I do not mean to lend currency to the impression that their roots do not firmly grip soil and subsoil as elsewhere. In the old world there is a strange dark bond that rivets human beings to the soil they plough up, which their fathers have ploughed up and cultivated before them. This bond or kinship bears with it a dusky sentiency; it is of a psychical reciprocity, close and warm and intimate, like one's own breath, indrawn and outgiven. Sometimes—Thomas Hardy's *Egdon Heath* is deeply illustrative—it wins a grim, elemental, half-human sway over the minor destinies of the people who dwell upon or around it. It is the stimulus, at moments, of passionate crime, stark and brutal, as a fell blow from behind, from ambush, leaving a rust-color upon the earth itself, for legend or poetry or fiction to use later on.

The American farmer does grasp the soil tensely, if only for the reason that, before the blazing onset of the pioneer, the earth was harsh and stony and overgrown with thick timber and weed and rank prairie grass. By dint of well-nigh superhuman effort, of hardship incredible, the forest and prairie blossomed in a gentle tilth, bore in good time rich fruit of corn and wheat and misty orchard. Yet when I try to probe the thoughts that animate those apparently intelligent critics who refer with contempt to the inhabitants of our so-called cornbelt in such terms as "hick," "yokel," "hayseed," "chawbacon," and so on, I find myself in no little perplexity. Palpably these sobriquets, too lightly flung out by the rather tired humorist, do not in the least suffice to fill in the canvas for us, to frame a concrete or revealing image, or to foreshadow, as we have every right to expect from criticism, a bare tithe of the problem, the complex of pressures, continually braved by small lonely communities drawing sustenance straight from the soil.

In one sense the European peasant may be said to be naïvely at peace with himself and his acres. Sleepily content at heart; hard-working and thrifty; at times bestially gross: so he lives on, essentially unawakened—even by the shock of the late war— harboring no troubling aims beyond the satisfaction, if what is soon sated can be called troublesome, of a few simple needs and appetites. Of the sombre ferment underlying repressed aspirations to soar above and beyond his inherited lot, there is little or no trace. Moreover, when we study the foreign peasant closer, we see that such insurgencies and bridlings as stir up the industrial classes to red rages everywhere convulse him not at all. In Russia today, for example, when he has been dealt with, or merely holds he has been dealt with, unjustly, he simply resorts to clandestine sabotage. On the other hand he does not, like the members of the middle estates, make peaceable but sturdy inroads into a higher social level. In Europe we have seen, of course, how a sudden revolution or an unsettling war may bring about overnight a complete realignment of the definite social zones; but this phenomenon, whenever it occurs, is chiefly restricted to the larger industrial centres, while the peasant, by reason of that obscure blood-kinship of which I have already spoken, remains immovably clenched to the land, as if to *la vraie verité.* In short, the tiller of the soil in Europe rarely evinces an active hankering to change his lot, to foist himself upon another stratum. When the earth proves to be obstinate, he may choose merely to migrate; but even to this step he is signally averse. Knut Hamsum's *Growth of the Soil* is, if we turn to it with the right temper of mind, the finely detailed saga of just this brooding, rock-rooted attachment to the eternal verity of the land.

In the United States, where farm-tenure is comparatively recent, we are faced with other conditions. Our type of commonwealth tends even in normal times to set by their heads all factions in the social and economic order; to cause them, despite their surface complacency, to be disgruntled and to chafe as at a bit. An unslackening winter of discontent rigidly grips our whole political and economic superstructure; and by this I do not refer to labour troubles alone, or to the just plaint made by the farmer touching prohibitive freight rates. The nerves of the nation, to change the figure, are being rawly prodded, as they were prodded long before the war, by the fatal knife of our own dominant fixed ideas. And these ideas, amounting pretty nearly to a creed, grew out of the hard conditions encountered by the first pioneers. In those days, if we read the chronicle of the pioneer aright, human conduct and personality were judged by the kind of effort put forth by the individual, his perseverance and single-mindedness, and the air of worldly competence with which he bore himself. These loomed up everywhere as noble and enviable traits. The unambitious, in a worldly sense, and the unpushing were accounted, as indeed they are now, spineless creatures, queer, feckless fellows, not worthy to be admitted into the hearty fellowship of the virile "go-getters" of that day and age. In certain states we have coined a term of deep opprobrium, as meaty to us as the older word "pariah" was to an older people, for this invertebrate or shiftless class; we call it—do we not?—"poor white".

What has been the direct effect on the farmer of this, our national drift toward an acquisitive civilization? To begin with, it has made him restive. No longer is it possible for him to view the nearby speculator with calm unruffled visage. And profounder evils, raw and sharp and subversive of his rumored sanity and level poise, have crept insidiously into his life. If he ever loved the soil, he no longer today regards it as anything more than an investment, a field for rigorous exploitation. But did he ever love it with the glowing loyalty the European feels for his paternal acres? It is extremely doubtful. Nowadays the American farmer does not enjoy the land; he has also lost sight of the niceties and spiritual delicacies of life: the comely vision of good living and sweetness and beauty in dwelling close to the earth. But have the women lost this keen zest for sweetness and beauty? Hardly. It is they who keep the flickering flame burning.

Thus we see that a huge segment of the rural population is nowise resigned to abide rural. It purposes, with a well-nigh vengeful doggedness accredited as praiseworthy in our tenor and type of civilization, to lift itself by hook or crook, by main contending force, into the blissful state of—

God save the mark!—the petty bourgeoisie. Of that vigorous foreign element scattered throughout the countryside in lumber camps, mines, and farms, little need be said here, for it is not quite germane to our argument. One-hundred-per-cent Americans, I daresay, are not always prone to concede that they are the new doughty pioneers. But what of that? Ask the poets! Always, everywhere, they flaunt a bit of rough earth-colour and so, in no slender degree, serve to enliven the drab peering interstices in the spread-out fabric of the American scene. Their quaint old-world customs are frequently seizable, as so many of our indigenous poets have long ago found out, as the pungent stuff of poetry. Notably Carl Sandburg, among others, with a newer moving rhythm has made lovely songs out of their winey dreams, their dim nostalgia, their uncouth dramas of the pick-and-shovel. Mark O'Dea in *Shivaree* has vividly drawn for us an inimitable portrait of a daughter of these people, although he does not give himself on this occasion to their poignant clashes with the new world, the alien environment.

In the following plays Mark O'Dea has gone elsewhere for his raw material: to those dull communities, desolate and mean and bare as a rain-washed wooden fence, which uncover no token of what we are pleased to call the cultural life; no theatres, no art museums, no amusements, indeed, save the dingy ice-cream parlor with its strident nickelodeon. For the older women, what remains outside of the clinging drudgery of household duties? Their spare hours, if they can

contrive somehow to filch any from the exactions
of the ox-like grind, are almost wholly given over
to vain chaperonage of the young, and the coy
sibilance of backyard innuendo and scandal. What
lonely spiritual wastes these small towns and town-
ships are! What sterile ponds coated over with
the opaque scum of ingrown desires and cadav-
erous hopes! Take our charted landscape from
seaboard to seaboard; let the hand fall where it
may. It will, nay, it is bound to alight upon
some such example of spiritual decay.

For the moment, as it happens, Mark O'Dea's
locale is an imaginary small town in Iowa. Any
cornbelt village of approximately the same size
and subject to the same general living conditions
is, inevitably, Red Bud. And what, precisely,
does Red Bud stand for among us today? It
stands for the stark empty lives of American farm
women; but for Mark O'Dea it stands also for
an awakening dimly astir in the consciousness of
these women. They reach out for new light; they
grope and totter and fall, half blinded by the
dazzle of the sudden sunshine; they seek to become
disinterested and gaze at life with but lately
opened eyes, searching for the beauty they have
hitherto so poignantly missed. They shudder
away from that vagueness of self which has been
so overwhelmingly their lot. But Red Bud, and
the world, to boot, thrusts them back, wounded,
fatally hurt, outlined stabbingly against the sur-
rounding bleakness.

These women of Red Bud—Mrs. Sykes, Miss
Myrtle, Miss Pansy, Ethelyn and, above all,

Hulda—gather within themselves, within their hungry or aroused or tormented souls, all the visionary escapements and sun-touched daydreams of half the women of present-day America. Here, beyond the outer rim of what we like to style the benefits of civilization, irradiated by not so much as a casual Chautauqua, one does not, it seems, even encounter the garrulous frou-frou of the culture or reading club. Meanwhile we are concerned, as Mark O'Dea so finely indicates, with the naked essentials of human existence, with the luminous end-of-the-road beckoning always and the balked will and the frustrate dream.

A short while ago in a magazine article, Mr. Joseph Hergesheimer advanced the thesis that women were in large part answerable for the widespread depraved or lush taste in reading to be found almost everywhere in the United States. I question the accuracy of this assertion. We might, if we chose, urge the very converse and come off just as triumphantly, if not beyond rebuttal. The real fault, if Mark O'Dea is to be believed, rests upon the shoulders of the men and is, in a sense— in a very large part, in fact—inherent in the cumulative factors that condition their lives. Of these soul-starved lives, we, who rush past in trains, can know but little. Yet we can get some slight idea of the devastating loneliness of the men and women who dwell in frontier settlements, where the pioneer with his Conestoga wagon camped, it seems, but yesterday, by evoking, by figuring to ourselves, the immense joy, as of the throwing up of a magic window, brought into these unlovely

houses by the bulky catalogue of a celebrated
mail-order house in Chicago. This pin-stitched
tome, containing several thousand pages brim-
ming with descriptive matter and illustrations,
sheds a little of the glamour that surrounds the
well-housed and well-clad dweller in big cities.

It may be granted Mr. Hergesheimer that the
woman on these farms, if she can get the leisure to
read at all, probably soaks up uncritically the
"glad books" of such authors as Harold Bell
Wright, Ethel M. Dell, and Gene Stratton Porter.
Mr. Hergesheimer, I need hardly point out, is
manifestly wrong when he puts the onus upon the
woman. Granted, too, her pliant softness for
roseate daydreams and the tailor-made hero of
the screen drama. The fault, if fault it is,
goes deeper into the tissue of the American
organism. And here O'Dea aids us considerably
in putting the question forthrightly. If no other
species of creative writing is capable of reaching
and awakening these women; if they can get
no emotional and esthetic purge from anything
except sugared bonbons and mawkish drivel,
where are we to fix the blame? Is it the environment, the prevailing atmosphere? Do the men on
the farms devote to the women half enough
thought? According to these plays, O'Dea holds
both the environment and the men to be chargeable.

For a number of years O'Dea lived amongst
the people he etches with such an unsparing hand
in his cycle of one-act plays. He has watched
closely their daily collision with the obdurate
forces hemming them about. But he is at bottom

a sympathetic familiar, not a cold, aloof, clinical analyst, of the half-sweet, half-bitter overtones of their existence. To him their hopes, their aspirations brim over with a childlike innocence and appeal. Why should it be so difficult to make this plain to certain dissectors of the American scene? Are they perhaps inveterate misogynists? And have they veiled their eyes so that they cannot see the truth for the jet filaments?

When I try to picture these women of Red Bud; Mrs. Sykes, who set her heart so desperately and so penetratingly on an electric lighting system; Miss Pansy, who seized the first available man as a husband; Miss Myrtle, who had vowed eternal hardness and whose spirit collapsed under the ironic pressure of events; Ethelyn, who groped for beauty in exaggerated cinema gestures and for whom "spooning" was an intriguing escapade; and finally the deliberate, embittered Hulda, who wed by way of protest—when, as I say, I try to picture these I behold numb aching faces behind the outward masks, faces athirst. Here are, if I mistake not, the pure contours of truth.

If O'Dea is a bit surgical, it will also be observed that he is essentially humane. If he were, on the other hand, a feminist special pleader—which he is not—it would have been a relatively simple matter to have painted the men villainously black. Carl Fishback and Solomon Sykes are hard men, gnarled, unwinning, but not unsympathetically portrayed. O'Dea is, or he chooses wisely to be, the artist rather than the propagandist. While he rarely departs from fidelity in character drawing, he strives, I suspect, for the epical, the broad-sweeping outline. And so it hardly astonishes us to find him not altogether committed to psychological detail, to an intense absorption in subconscious motives as is, for example, Sherwood Anderson. He is, however, somewhat allured by the emphasis and point of sheer situation. Perhaps he remembers his Flaubert and his Maupassant. In any case, sheer human situation may still claim its rightful prerogative today, especially with us in America.

O'Dea has deliberately chosen the one-act play as his medium. And wisely, I believe. Since he was at the outset drawn to dramatic form, this medium is most expedient since it exacts fewer concessions in the shaping and reshaping of original material. I shall be told, no doubt, by so-called students of the theatre that the one-act play is more demanding than the three- or four-act play and, eventually, rather futile. No greater absurdity was ever spoken! The whole trend of the modern theatre is toward strictest simplification and, what is more, toward a rather loose extension of the brief single act mould. For witness, we need but point to the recent work of Eugene O'Neill, George Kaiser, and Walter Hasenclever.

If O'Dea continues to work in this form, he is bound, ultimately, to achieve self-integration. And this is the highest goal of all creative spirits, who seek to give us observed reality after it has been steeped in the solution of fluid personal vision. And for this purpose the one-act play, or some such form of it, as let us say, *The Hairy Ape*, commends itself as at once superior to the graver architectonic formulary of three or four acts.

The drama, along with other literary and esthetic forms, is becoming more and more personal in its expression, as spontaneously personal, I had almost said, as the concise lyric. This tendency is visible in O'Dea's work. Thus it is that, while he is always realistic, he has not flung off a series of Zolaesques against the American backdrop. The plays are not starkly veristic, for all their fidelity to the matter in hand, in the sense in which, say, the Sicilian, Giovanni Verga, who also wrote about peasant life (another brand of peasant life, to be sure!) is commonly taken to be so. They are not chaotic; there is a sane regard for translation into dramatic effect; for unity of emotion is, clearly, the due end sought.

On laying down the present book the reader may perhaps conclude that the problem of modern America is intertangled with the problem of the American woman. And to a large extent this is true. The foreigner who pays us a flying visit usually insists that the average American wife and "flapper" are pampered and petted beyond belief and reason. H. L. Mencken, nearer home, also firmly holds that women occupy an ascendant position among us; that we are, in fact, wilting under a fragrant assault of petticoat government in public and domestic life. Here and there, amongst our leisure classes, this may be substantiated. But is it tenable about even half of our feminine population? Is it true regarding the women of such places as Red Bud?

Mr. Mencken goes on to say: "Nowhere in the world have women more leisure and freedom to improve their minds and nowhere else do they show a higher level of intelligence or take part more effectively in affairs of first importance." Obviously, no matter what we think of the "intelligence" of American women, this pronouncement does not apply to the womenfolk on our outpost farms. Mr. W. L. George is, I believe, far closer to the mark when he asserts that Europe does not as yet comprehend the status of the American woman. It is naturally prone to draw summary conclusions from the well-to-do examples who tour Europe once a year for pleasure. It knows nothing of the archaic conditions which surround those who are compelled to live on solitary farms. Is the American woman sybaritic, preying, and idle? For the reader who is, it may be, still mazed in doubt, Mark O'Dea in the present cycle of one-act plays volunteers a hint of the final, irrefutable answer.

PIERRE LOVING.

San Francisco, Calif.
April, 1922.

THE SONG OF SOLOMON

PERSONS IN THE PLAY

SOLOMON SYKES, *a Farmer*
MARY SYKES, *his Wife*
MRS. SMITHERS,
MRS. BAMBERGER, } *Neighbors*
MR. KERNS, *the Minister*

THE SONG OF SOLOMON was presented for the first time by the Arts Club of Chicago, November 9, 1920.

THE SONG OF SOLOMON

There is one farm just outside of Red Bud which always commands the admiration of passers-by. Beyond the well-kept fencing, past the productive fields, the eye wanders to the unusually fine buildings.

The barn is particularly large, really monumental, with towering silos. There are numerous buildings, all spick and span, grouped around this "show" barn. An estate, one surmises. And one looks for a handsome house, rising midst the small grove of trees.

Were one to wander into the lane that stretches quite a distance from the highway and approach this group of buildings, one would be disappointed in not finding a palatial home.

For the house is a low, built-on affair that has just grown from a tiny cottage into a larger. It is conspicuously inappropriate midst the grandeur of its surroundings. Yet it is not a hovel. It is a comfortable enough old house, possibly not such a misfit on the average farm, but long since entirely inadequate for such a place as this.

For years this farm has been "a steady earner." Its owner, Solomon Sykes, is rated as one of the richest farmers in the community. Year after year he has improved it, yet he has always banked a portion of each year's yield. In this way he has built up a secondary income—his banker has recommended farm mortgages, and many farms in the county, and beyond, pay interest to Mr. Sykes.

But people say that he is "a hard man to get along with." He has always been "mighty tight-mouthed." Nobody knows his resources, not even his family. He is not altogether a miser, but the years of hard work in developing this farm have made him extremely cautious, and, having always been dependent upon self, he is as thrifty as he is industrious.

He is proud of his farm. He is proud of his position in the community. He is proud of having "riz his family right" and of having set up his sons on neighboring farms.

But he is strangely negligent as to personal comforts. He has forgotten to build a home, or he has just been putting it off year after year. A new house has always been "next year" for a long, long time. For every year there has been something else, and always that something else has meant more acreage, or finer cattle, or additional machinery, or tiling, or anything but a house.

Until now . . . there are just two of them, Mr. and Mrs. Sykes, and they are getting along in years and the old house has sheltered a bigger family when the children were at home. And it is a "sorta comfortable-like" place. And its a big job "to up and build a new house with all these new-fangled idees."

"But I'd think," says Mrs. Smithers to Mrs. Bamberger, "that Sol Sykes would be ashamed of such an old rattle-trap." They are walking down the lane toward the house on this hot July morning. "And so would I," agrees Mrs. Bamberger, " 'cause he's so proud and highty-tighty."

As they approach the house, their conversation becomes more quiet and confidential. As they come around the side of the house to the rear, we again pick up the thread of their gossip.

The back porch and the yard are not very well kept; in fact, this is the worst part of the farm, the greatest contrast. Through the back porch we can see into the kitchen, a big, old-fashioned room with a large range. Out in the yard, on one side of the porch, are a wash-bench, with tubs on it and an old washing-machine. Opposite are an old grindstone, a rickety bench, and a discarded milk stool. There is also a dilapidated, weather-beaten rocking-chair.

There is little grass—the yard is worn down to the bare earth around the porch. But the spot is shady and inviting on such a hot morning, and Mrs. Smithers and Mrs. Bamberger have planned to make it an oasis on their journey over to the harvesting.

They are middle-aged farm women, dressed in their everyday clothes of wash-goods. Mrs. Smithers is rather sour and peppery, while Mrs. Bamberger is motherly and genial.

As they come round the house, Mrs. Smithers is telling Mrs. Bamberger "the latest."

MRS. SMITHERS

Well, I heard that Mis' Jones said that she wouldn't let her daughter marry him, even if he did come back.

MRS. BAMBERGER

My goodness! Has he skipped out?

MRS. SMITHERS

Yes, didn't you hear that? Well, I'll tell you what I heard Mis' McIntire say—you know she knows his sister. Well, she said he'd be willin' to marry her if—'s-sh, I'll tell you later. (*They reach the back of the house and come into view.*) I wonder where Mis' Sykes is. I'll jest look in her kitchen. No, she ain't there—mebbe she's upstairs. Oh, I'm so hot, ain't you? Let's set down a minute and cool off. (*They go over to the bench and sit down. Mrs. Smithers leans over confidentially.*) Have you noticed anything queer about Mis' Sykes?

MRS. BAMBERGER

Queer? No, nothin' particular. Have you?

MRS. SMITHERS

Well, no, can't say as I have. But people —well, some are sorta wonderin'—you know she don't come to church any more.

MRS. BAMBERGER

She ain't been very well lately. Sorta porely-like.

MRS. SMITHERS

Yes, I know, but—

MRS. BAMBERGER

She's allus readin' her Bible, ain't she, even if she don't go to meetin's.

MRS. SMITHERS

Yes, but—

MRS. BAMBERGER

Well . . .?

MRS. SMITHERS

I didn't mean to tell you—but don't you tell nobody—now.

MRS. BAMBERGER

No, I won't.

MRS. SMITHERS

Well, she has been sorta queer-like lately.

MRS. BAMBERGER

You mean more'n usual for a woman that's growin' on 60?

MRS. SMITHERS

Yes, some one told me. Oh, I don't know whether I should repeat it or not.

MRS. BAMBERGER

I promised not to tell.

MRS. SMITHERS

Well, this is what I heard. Folks as has been passin' by say Mis' Sykes has been screamin' something terrible—right in the middle of the day—when she was all alone here—when the men folks were in the field. Oh, such awful screams—like as if she was bein' murdered.

MRS. BAMBERGER

Does Sol Sykes know it?

MRS. SMITHERS

No.

MRS. BAMBERGER

How do you know?

MRS. SMITHERS

Folks have sorta hinted to him, askin' if she was well, and the likes. He allus says she is the same as ever.

7

MRS. BAMBERGER

Well, that ain't proof that he don't know.

MRS. SMITHERS

If he knows, he's keepin' it a secret. But I'm sure he don't know. Men are so wrapped up in farmin'—you know how it is. They don't pay any 'tention to such things—like as not if he heered it in the distance, as he comes up to the house, he'd think it singin'. And she'd be keerful to stop when she saw him comin'.

MRS. BAMBERGER

Well, if that's all there is to it, he'll find out sooner or later. Howsoever, I don't believe there's a word of truth in it, do you? She's jest the same as ever, so far as I know. I never seen her do anything queer. And I like Mis' Sykes; she's been a mighty good neighbor for all these years. Why, when I had Jessie, and that doctor was away gallivantin' in the next county, it was Mis' Sykes as come right in and took his place. I'll never fergit *that* to my dyin' day.

MRS. SMITHERS

Yes, she's a mighty good Methodist.

MRS. BAMBERGER

Methodist? What's that gotta do with her takin' care of me and my baby?

MRS. SMITHERS

Well, I jest meant that she was kind to everybody.

MRS. BAMBERGER

You bet she is. And if anybody says to me that she's actin' queer-like, I know what I'll say to them, the busybodies! And you stop such

8

talk—now won't you, Mis' Smithers, please do. It ain't right.

MRS. SMITHERS

Well, I don't know whether to believe it or not. It seems so strange.

MRS. BAMBERGER

I wonder *where* she is. Mebbe I'd better call her or go into—

(*Mrs. Sykes's voice is heard as she comes to the kitchen door. She comes to the edge of the porch with the Bible in her hand, reading. She does not see her visitors at first. They sit, transfixed in astonishment. She is a person of sixty, a little thin woman, with tightly-combed white hair. She is in a calico wrapper, with an apron. She epitomizes at a glance her sixty years of work on the farm, her privations, her drudgery. There is infinite sadness in her face, immeasurable pathos. What she reads, however, is not in her natural tone. It seems strangely reminiscent of youth. It is only after finishing it that one is struck with its unnaturalness, as she lapses into her everyday life.*)

MRS. SYKES

"My beloved is white and ruddy, the chiefest among ten thousand.

His head is as the most fine gold, his locks are bushy and black as a raven.

His eyes are as the eyes of doves by the rivers of water, washed with milk, and fitly set.

His cheeks are as a bed of spices, as sweet flowers.

9

His lips like lilies, dropping with sweet myrrh.
His hands are as gold rings set with the beryl;
his . . ."

MRS. SMITHERS (*in a whisper*)
The Song of Solomon!

(*Mrs. Sykes stops. She has heard the whisper and glances around as in a trance, until she suddenly sees her visitors. She is embarrassed, hiding her Bible under her apron, not knowing just what to do or say. She is as a person caught in the act of doing something wrong.*)

MRS. SYKES
Why—why—I never knew you were here! I —well, I—

MRS. BAMBERGER
Oh, we jest was goin' over to the threshin' to help at the cook wagon, gettin' dinner . . . . and we got so hot we jest thought we'd drop in fer a minute and see you. We jest come.

MRS. SYKES
You jest come?

MRS. SMITHERS
Yes, jest this minute.

MRS. SYKES
I must git you a glass of water.

MRS. BAMBERGER
Now, don't, Mis' Sykes, don't bother. Jest set down here with us a bit. How are you these days? The heat's perty bad, ain't it, Mis' Sykes?

MRS. SMITHERS

I think the dust is worse, and the flies. I said to Mr. Smithers—

MRS. SYKES

I keep pretty well. You know I'm never sick. Just bilious-like onct in a while. But not much lately. (*To Mrs. Smithers.*) Are *you* bilious, Mis' Smithers? Sody's good.

MRS. SMITHERS

Well, I ain't exactly bilious. But I got something like it. Seems I allus got somethin' or other. I'm mighty porely, you know. I jest git so tired takin all that medicine; it never seems to do any good. 'Pears to me like I've sampled 'em all in the drug-store. Somebody said I orta take up Christian Science.

(*This revolutionary thought creates astonishment.*)

MRS. BAMBERGER

Why, Mis' Smithers, what an idee!

MRS. SYKES

Christian Science? You? Such a good Methodist?

MRS. SMITHERS

Well, I jest said somebody said I *orta*. That's no sign I am.

MRS. BAMBERGER

But how kin you even mention it? It gives decent folks such a start. (*Just then the Bible falls from under Mrs. Sykes's apron, right on the ground in front of them all. She picks it up hurriedly, in confusion.*) If you'd read your Bible, like Mis' Sykes, you'd be better off.

MRS. SMITHERS (*cattishly*)

Readin' what *she* reads?

(*Mrs. Bamberger glares at her. Mrs. Sykes looks questioningly at the two women as if she must say something to justify the reading of The Song of Solomon.*)

MRS. SYKES

Maybe you don't understand.

MRS. BAMBERGER

Understand? Why, you don't have to explain, Mis' Sykes.

(*Mrs. Smithers gives a disdainful grunt.*)

MRS. SYKES

Maybe *you* want to know, Mis' Smithers, why I'm readin' The Song of Solomon?

MRS. SMITHERS (*rather sourly*)

Well, it strikes me as a peculiar part to be readin'.

MRS. SYKES

Peculiar? Why, it's the loveliest part of the Bible! (*This is indeed scandalous, as the looks of the two visitors show.*) I read it every anniversary!

MRS. BAMBERGER AND MRS. SMITHERS

Anniversary?

MRS. SYKES

Yes. To-day's our weddin' anniversary. Sol and me's been married now forty-three years—forty-three years—forty-three years.

(*This she repeats slowly, as though the whole panorama of the past were flashing by. The visitors*

12

watch her as she gazes off into space, rather trance-like.)

MRS. SMITHERS (*addressing Mrs. Bamberger*)
I don't see the point, do you?

MRS. SYKES (*as if coming back to consciousness of her surroundings*)
I don't mind telling you, sence you're such old friends. *Some* folks wouldn't understand. But *you* will.

MRS. BAMBERGER (*gently*)
Sure, we will, Mis' Sykes. You jest tell us all about your weddin' anniversary and The Song of Solomon.

MRS. SMITHERS
I would certainly like to know, bein' as we all belong to the same congregation.

MRS. SYKES
Well, the church is got a lot to do with it. Not our new church. But the one that stood in its place forty-three years ago—so long ago—so long ago. Why, I was seventeen, then, and it was jest such a day as this, a beautiful day. It was a Sunday mornin', jest about this hour. . . .

(*Mrs. Sykes gains in spirit, becoming more alert, less tired looking. A stray sun-shaft pierces the shadows and il'umines her face, somewhat enlivening her ashen complexion. She looks years younger.*)

I had known the Sykes since I was a child. One of the boys had allus been sorta nice to me, but it never meant nothin' to me. I didn't understand. Our family and the Sykes family

were at church that mornin'. One of the Sykes
boys sat next to me. I liked him that mornin'
as we sat there, listenin' to the sermon. Then
came the long, silent prayer. They used to
be longer than they are now. And we prayed
on our knees, too. Jest when we got ready to
pray—the awfulest thing happened! That
Sykes boy opened a Bible and put it down
right in front of me. He pointed to it, so
friendly-like. It was The Song of Solomon.
And it was Solomon Sykes that handed me that
Bible. Of course, I should have closed it and
gone on prayin'. But somethin' within me—
some sort of spirit—glued my eyes to the pages.
I read on. I read on. It was a revelation. I
grew from a girl to a woman there in that
church, with my head bowed down as if in
prayer. I dared not look up. I couldn't. I
felt as if I wanted to walk out of that church
with my eyes shut, and go to some place all by
myself and think—and think. When the prayer
was over, I sat there as in a trance. I never
heard another word of the services. At the end
I got up, hopin' to get out easily, but knowin'
that Sol was watchin' me every minute. When
we got to the door, he came to me—there with
my family around—and asked, jest as polite-like
as if nothin' had happened, if he could see me
home in his buggy. And I went. We rode off
in silence—nary a word. But we didn't go far.
We came to the walnut grove—long sence cut
down. We got out—I seemed to obey as if some
power controlled me. We went and set down

there in the woods. Then he popped the question right there. And I said I'd be his wife. I can't tell you *all* about it—that I will keep my own secret—maybe it wasn't so different from other proposals, but it allus seemed so to *me*. Because we talked about The Song of Solomon. He said it was as if writ for *us*. And so we were married—forty-three years ago. And every anniversary I read The Song of Solomon. It takes me back over this long, long happiness; it brings back all that God has give me. He is good. He has been so good to me. And to my Sol and to my children. And to everybody. (*Mrs. Bamberger is crying. Mrs. Smithers is in a nervous quandary.*) Oh, friends, let us pray— let us pray.

MRS. SMITHERS
Not here in the yard, surely?

MRS. SYKES
Why not? All is God. God is all.

MRS. SMITHERS (*fidgeting*)
I think we'd better be goin'. Don't you, Mis' Bamberger?

(*Mrs Sykes gazes abstractedly into space, as if her mind has again gone back to that Sunday morning so many years ago. Mrs. Bamberger sits subdued, wiping her tears away. She then rises and goes over to Mrs. Sykes, putting her arm around her shoulder.*)

MRS. BAMBERGER
I understand, Mis' Sykes, *I* understand.

(*Mrs. Sykes looks at her appreciatively, realiz-*

*ing that here is a friend indeed, a friend who un-
derstands.*)

MRS. SYKES

You understand?

MRS. BAMBERGER

Yes, yes, I understand. You and me will talk
about it again some time. But now, we must
be goin'.

(*Mrs. Sykes comes out of her reminiscent mood
quickly, becoming the solicitous hostess again.*)

MRS SYKES.

I *must* get you a drink. Jest a minute. I'll
fetch some.

MRS. BAMBERGER

No. Let *me*.

(*Mrs. Bamberger goes into kitchen, and returning
with pail and tin cup, passes a drink to each.*)

MRS. SMITHERS

Heared Mr. Sykes was gonna buy a tractor.

MRS. SYKES (*surprised*)

A tractor? Oh, no, that's a mistake. He ain't
gonna buy one. Why, they cost over a thousand dollars. Besides, we got all those horses
which we gotta have for cultivatin'. Tractor's
mostly for plowin'. We couldn't have the
horses standin' 'round eatin their heads off most
of the year, jest to do the cultivatin' and odd
jobs. A tractor ain't like horses. Ain't handy
enough. Jest good for plowin'.

MRS. SMITHERS

Well, I heered my husband tell one of the hands

that the salesman told him that Mr. Sykes had been talkin' pretty seriously.

MRS. BAMBERGER (*noting Mrs. Sykes's worry*)
Oh, it's jest probably talk, nothin' else. Mis' Sykes orta know.

MRS. SYKES
I'd rather have a 'lectric lightin' plant, one of them new riggins. They don't cost as much, neither. Only about four hundred dollars.

MRS. SMITHERS
Yes, but that ain't *all*. The salesman told my husband that the wirin' cost a lot. And Mr. Smithers says to me, he says: "Well, even that ain't all. If I bought one of those rigs I'd have to put in a bathroom and all the plumbin'. I'd have to buy a 'lectric washin' machine," he says. "And a 'lectric iron. And rig it up with a tank so's to have running water right in the house. And a sink in the kitchen. Well," my husband says, "It would be jest like livin' in the city." And I jest kept at him, so now he's gonna buy one right after harvest. No more lamps! No more trapesin' outa doors in all kinds of weather to the pump. Runnin' water! And a bathtub! And lights out in the yard! And at the barn! I tell you, it's great!

(*During this oration Mrs. Sykes listens eagerly, like a child thrilled at some marvelous description of a coming circus.*)

MRS. SYKES
Oh, it must be wonderful!

17

MRS. SMITHERS

Yes, and I'd think *you'd* be the first to have one.
Why, they're puttin' 'em in all over the country.   Here, you've got the finest farm in the
neighborhood, fine fencin' and barns and cattle
and an ottamobile and everything *else*.   I say
to Mrs. Smithers that I want to enjoy things as I
go along.   Shrouds ain't got no pockets.   We
can't take our money with us when we pass on.
Why, I was readin' one of them advertisements,
and it was headed: "FREE YOURSELF FROM
HOUSEHOLD DRUDGERY."   And it showed pitchers of how a 'lectric plant eased a body's work.
And it's jest a little gasoline engine and some
'lectrical fixin's, all sorta small, an' it goes right
in the cellar and runs itself.   I think it's jest
like magic.

MRS. BAMBERGER

We *must* be gittin' along.

MRS. SMITHERS

It makes me mad that city wimmen's got all
sech and think nothin' of it.   I tell you if
them suffragettes that go paradin' around
would jest spend their time and money helpin'
their sisters on the farm, it would do more for
us than votes ever can.   We don't need to be
trained to vote as much as our men folks need
to be trained how to loosen up a little around
the house.   Why, the house is always the very
last thing—everything else comes first with the
men.   One gits in a livable house jest about
when one's gittin' ready to lay down in a

coffin. It ain't right! I says to Mr. Smithers,
I says—

MRS. BAMBERGER

We *must* go, Mis' Smithers.

MRS. SMITHERS

Yes, we must go. Good-bye, Mis' Sykes. You
must come over an' see me. I want to tell you
what *I* said to Mr. Smithers when *he* said to
me that—

MRS. BAMBERGER

Good-bye, Mis' Sykes. I'm comin' in to see
you again soon. Many happy returns of the
day. Come, Mis' Smithers.

MRS. SMITHERS

Oh, I fergot. Yes, many happy returns of the
day, Mis' Sykes. Good-bye.

MRS. SYKES

Good-bye, Mis' Bamberger. Good-bye, Mis'
Smithers. Come again.

(*Mrs. Sykes sits down in the weather-beaten rocking-chair and rocks back and forth with a happy expression. One doesn't know whether she is thinking about The Song of Solomon or the electric plant.
Finally she opens the Bible and begins reading
again.*)

MRS. SYKES

"Set me as a seal upon thine heart, and as a
seal upon thine arm, for love is strong as death,
My beloved is—"

(Mr. Sykes comes around the corner of the house with the mail. He is a little, old man, bent with years of labor. He is in work clothes.)

MR. SYKES

Hello, Mary, here's the mail. Not much. No letters from the children. Is dinner ready? *(He notes the open Bible on her lap.)* Ain't you readin' the Bible an awful lot lately, Mary? How do you find time?

MRS. SYKES

Dinner? Is it time? *(She pauses.)* Yes, I got it cookin'. Some things bilin'. *(But she does not get up. She merely sits, while he looks over the mail, opening a newspaper.)* Sol, do you know what day this is?

MR. SYKES

Friday, ain't it?

MRS. SYKES

Oh, I don't mean that.

MR. SYKES *(examining the date-line of the paper)*

Well, it's the ninth, then.

MRS. SYKES

Sol—Sol—have you fergot what day this is?

MR. SYKES

What's the matter? What do you mean?

MRS. SYKES

This is our weddin' anniversary!

MR. SYKES

Oh, that's what you mean. *(Goes on reading the paper.)*

MRS. SYKES *(wistfully)*

You didn't fergit, did you, Sol? *(It dawns

*on her that he has forgotten, as he shows his lack
of interest, his refuge in the newspaper. There is
an air of futility, of helpless hopes, of resigna-
tion. She shakes her head, folds her hands, and
rocks, as Sol stolidly resists any sentimental appeal.)* Sol—Sol—

MR. SYKES *(somewhat petulantly)*
Well—well, what is it now?

MRS. SYKES
You ain't gonna buy a tractor, are you?

MR. SYKES
Mebbe.

MRS. SYKES
Instead of a 'lectric-lightin' plant?

MR. SYKES
Yes, mebbe I am.

MRS. SYKES
Oh, Sol, we don't need a tractor like as we need
the 'lectric plant. We orta have more home
comforts now, while we're livin'. We ain't gotta
make more money. We got all we need. Jest
for us two. The children's all taken care of.

MR. SYKES
Them new-fangled notions ain't to my likin'.

MRS. SYKES
A 'lectric plant's no more new-fangled than a
tractor. And the tractor costs three times as
much as the 'lectric plant, and won't bring us
half as much comfort. We're gittin old, Sol.
My heart is set on havin' some comforts before
we pass on. We've—I can't go on this way—
I jest can't. I ain't got the strength any more.

MR. SYKES

We could get the 'lectric plant *after* we git the tractor.

MRS. SYKES

It's allus *after*, allus *after*. Seems I've heard that all my life. Allus *after*. And *after* ain't come *yit*.

MR. SYKES

Well, I've ordered the tractor!

(*This is a terrific surprise, a bitter disappointment. It dashes the final hope to pieces. It recalls all its precedents. Mrs. Sykes is moved beyond words.*)

MRS. SYKES (*chokingly*)
Sol—Sol—

(*He reads, knowing that he has ended his talk, secure in his brutality. Mrs. Sykes walks into the house in a daze—reeling somewhat, as if faint. As she enters the kitchen, restrained, choking sobs are heard. Around the corner of the house appears Rev. Kerns, the Red Bud shepherd of the Methodist flock. He is a pompous, oratorical person of about thirty-five, though rather direct and business-like.*)

MR. KERNS

How'd do, Brother Sykes, how'd do?

MR. SYKES

Good mornin', Mr. Kerns.

MR. KERNS

I just met Sister Smithers—a fine woman, a real Christian soul. And Sister Smithers said

22

(*unctuously*) that this was your wedding anniversary.

MR. SYKES
Yes, it is.

MR. KERNS
Well, that's fine. My congratulations, Brother Sykes, my congratulations. How many years is it now that you and Sister Sykes have been mated in the holy bonds of matrimony?

MR. SYKES (*embarrassed, for he does not know*)
Well, it's been a long time. Now let me see—you know I ain't good at figgers—let me see—my wife allus knows—well, I guess it's bin at least forty-five years. Or is it forty-four?

MR. KERNS
You have been an example to the community, Brother Sykes—you and Sister Sykes. We're proud of you. Yes, people look up to you. You have set a good example of how a man and wife should live. How satisfied you must feel, how— . . .

MR. SYKES (*flattered*)
Well, I allus believed in livin' accordin' to the Holy Writ. I—

MR. KERNS
If all our folks set an example like you—

MR. SYKES
I believe in old-fashioned religion and the Ten Commandments. I believe . . .

(*Unseen by the men, Mrs. Sykes comes to the door, and overhears the conversation.*)

MR. KERNS
Yes, I know your beliefs, Mr. Sykes. But what

I wanted to see you about this morning in particular—in addition to congratulating you—was the improvements on the church. I came to you first of all the deacons, knowing that you'd set an example. Your share, according to your standing, is about five hundred dollars. And I know you'll want to give it, as a sort of anniversary offering.

MR. SYKES

Five hundred dollars! Ain't that purty steep?

MR. KERNS

No, not for *you*. Think how it will impress the others. It will make them liberal, too. (*Mrs. Sykes comes out into the yard, and to their notice.*) Why, how'd do, Sister Sykes, congratulations! (*She is pleased, looking at Mr. Sykes, thinking he has told the minister.*) Sister Smithers just told me. (*Mrs. Sykes is thoroughly disappointed.*)

MRS. SYKES

Thanks!

MR. KERNS

Brother Sykes has just promised—or as well as promised—I mean he has practically agreed—to give the church five hundred dollars for the improvements. And I said this was a happy day to do it—sort of an anniversary offering.

MRS. SYKES

Sol, kin you afford it?

MR. SYKES (*proudly*)

Yes, I kin afford it. I'll do it. (*To the minister.*) An' you make the others give, too. Let's make the church finer than ever. I believe in

a house of worship as is a credit to the community. And I donate this five hundred dollars in honor of our weddin' anniversary.

(*This afterthought he directs to his wife, expecting her to be thrilled by it and forget her other
ideas. In his mind it justifies the selection of
the tractor.*)

MR. KERNS

Oh, thank you, Brother Sykes. Thank you,
Sister Sykes. It is a noble spirit. That is true
love. How happy it must make you, Sister
Sykes, to have such a fine husband—such a true
mate. Thank you, thank you. I must spread
the good news. I must hasten to the others.
Thank you again. And now, good-bye, my
friends. Good-bye. You have done a good
deed to-day. And God is with you. Good-bye.

MR. SYKES

Good-bye, Mr. Kerns. (*To Mrs. Sykes, who
has sunk into the chair.*) Say "Good-bye,"
Mary.

MRS. SYKES (*sadly, monotonously*)

Good-bye, good-bye.

(*Mr. Kerns goes out.*)

MR. SYKES

Ain't you proud of my anniversary present,
Mary?

MRS. SYKES (*meditatively, but not in reply*)

The five hundred dollars to the church—the
thousand dollars for the tractor—nothin',
nothin' for *me*. No, I ain't proud. I allus come
after everything else. And I'm feared *after*

25

is too late—too late.   Every time I git robbed.
Somethin' comes along and takes things away
from me jest as I am gittin' ready for them.

MR. SYKES (*disappointed and cranky*)

I can't understand you, Mary.   Are you still
thinkin' about that 'lectric-lightin' plant and
all the fixin's for the house?   Might as well put
it off'n your mind, fer we can't do all that this
year.   Mebbe next.

(*Mrs. Sykes sits rocking nervously in her chair.
She pulls her Bible out from underneath her apron.
She acts as if she is about to read it.   But in-
decision is in control.   She looks helplessly about,
even frantically.   Her eyes wander crazily hither
and thither.   Mr. Sykes, giving a gesture of
"What's the use?" goes into the house.   Mrs. Sykes's
face twitches and her paleness seems to turn a gray-
green.   Some sun-shaft or reflection silhouettes her
shrunken face and faded hair in ghastly hid-
eousness.   Her slow rocking becomes faster, then
diminishes.   Slowly she crumples and shrinks in
the chair, seeming to collapse.   Suddenly there is
a low, chuckling, fiendish gurgle, a silly laugh—
a horrible, inarticulate, sputtering sound.   As if
electrocuted, her body stiffens, hurls itself up, spins
around.   A blood-curdling scream—that age-
old announcement of departing reason.   A pene-
trating, marrow-freezing scream, ending in the
choking gurgle.   She falls to her knees, then to
her elbows.   She beats the ground as she moans.
Her thin hair falls over her scrawny neck.*)

CURTAIN

SHIVAREE

PERSONS IN THE PLAY

JOHN, *the Groom*
HULDA, *the Bride*
SIM ⎱
MILLY ⎰ *Friends*

SHIVAREE was presented for the first time at the Cameo
Theatre, Chicago, February 23, 1922.

SHIVAREE

It is a soft, June night on an Iowa farm. Earlier in the evening there has been a wedding in the neighborhood.

Many a June has passed since such an important marriage. The parents of the bride and groom own the largest farms in the county—farms which, through years of labor and thrift, have been developed from the clearings of pioneers into the highly productive acreages of today, the showplaces of Red Bud township.

As if it were a royal match, uniting two vast domains, John Poff's father—John is the groom—has always felt that such a marriage was advantageous. He has seen to it that the land he has helped John to buy adjoins a rich "eighty" owned by Hulda's father. In fact, John's father has supervised personally the amorous adventures of his son, reducing them to a safe minimum which would insure John's inevitable selection of the desirable Hulda.

John has inherited much of this canniness and has grown to manhood rather more practical than romantic. Yet this spirit of father and son is no different from that of their neighbors, an inheritance passed on through generations of struggle with the soil and with the capricious elements of nature. Hulda's father, too, has welcomed the idea of such an alliance. He knows that John is a first-rate farmer, one who will be interested always in a growing bank account rather than anything else.

John has built the new farmhouse—a square, boxlike structure, devoid of architectural grace. He and Hulda have furnished it, but they have depended largely upon the wedding gifts of parents, relatives, and friends, which accounts for the hodge-podge of interior adornment.

Throughout the preparation of this future home, John's chief interest has been concentrated on barns and machinery, fields and stock. He has been perfectly willing to let "the wimmen-folks" fuss with the interior decoration of the house.

The furniture is mostly Golden Oak, which stands out glowingly against the white plastered walls, later, when soiled, to be papered with some of that "pretty rose design, to match the carpet," as Hulda has suggested.

There is a stark barrenness about the rooms, due partly to the glaring walls and partly to the lack of curtains, which will not be put up until fall, "because they ketch the dust so." The green shades stand out boldly.

However, the bedroom is cosier, for it is decked in flowers. Had there been any "set pieces," one might have mistaken the elaborate display as belonging to a funeral, flowers being usually more plentiful in Red Bud when folks are "laid away" than when they are married.

The bedroom boasts a massive brass bed, and the dresser has a "swell front," according to the description in a prominent mail-order catalogue. On a table is an acetylene lamp with a shade of pressed red glass, to resemble a rose—though of cabbage-size proportion.

Outside, noise and din are heard, a typical countryside charivari—the culmination of nuptial ceremonies near Red Bud. The bedroom evidently has an entrance door from the outside, for it opens with a crash, as the bride and groom enter, he first. The crowd surges to the door. John slams it shut and locks it. The noise increases and continues, as the revellers bring their celebration to a climax.

John is rather small, rather thin, rather leathery in complexion, with none of the brilliant coloring noted in Hulda. He wears the "conventional black," with a narrow, white bow-knot tie. His hair is carefully plastered down.

In fact, John might easily be mistaken for other than an Iowa farmer. One can almost imagine him as a prim bookkeeper in the big city, until he identifies himself with the soil by his speech.

Then one notes his large hands and his slight stoop and ambling stride, and one pictures him following the plow and plodding along over the soft furrows. His face has little expression. He is endeavoring nobly to rise to the occasion, but it is difficult. He wishes the "whole durned thing" were over, for he has lost several precious days from the fields.

Hulda is gowned in wedding splendor—a strapping woman, heroic in figure, with dangling hands. She walks like a giantess, swinging her awkward arms. She is much taller than John—a big woman in every way.

31

Strangely, she has none of the calm that usually accompanies such a figure. She is flushed with excitement, but the situation—the escape from the celebration—seems to quiet her. She assumes a questioning look however, gazing around the room and glancing nervously at her new husband.

She is perplexed. The safety of the crowded day is past. As though she had forgotten to prepare for such an occasion as this, she apparently does not know what to do next.

Furthermore, she is exhausted. She would like to sit down and take off her shoes—they are so tight. She has suffered all day, shifting her weight first to one foot, then to the other, yearning, even during the ceremony, for the time when she could rest her aching feet.

Such a very large woman and such a very little man offer a strange contrast as they stand there for a moment, listening to the "shivaree," embarrassed, hesitant, confused.

JOHN (*jubilantly*)

Wow, but that was a humdinger! I thought I'd die laughin' the way they carried on.

HULDA (*slowly, solemnly*)

I wish they'd go.

JOHN

What fer?

(*He flits around the room, thoroughly excited by the events of the evening. Hulda goes to a chair and sits down stiffly, as though she were a caller in a strange house. She glances surreptitiously*

32

around the room—but most of the time gazes into space.)

JOHN
Why, that was the gol-durndest shivaree—gosh, did you ever hear such noise? And the way the boys cut up! I tell you, Huldie, we orta be mighty proud. I never seen the likes. Didn't *you* think it was grand?

HULDA
No, I don't like shivarees.

JOHN (*surprised*)
Don't like shivarees! What do you mean? The finest ever given in Red Bud County? Aw, you're jest done up.

HULDA
That ain't it. I don't like 'em.

JOHN
Why not?

HULDA
I'm feared you wouldn't understand, but—

(Just then some of the merrymakers came to the window and play rat-a-tat-tat. Hulda starts up nervously, leaving her seat to walk about. A gesture of dislike is apparent as she shuts out the noise by putting her hands over her ears. John stalks proudly to the window and pulls down the shade. Then the other shades. He laughs and is delighted with this demonstration. From now on the charivari party is heard to depart in its caravan of flivvers, with noises and clatter gradually diminishing. Hulda takes her seat again. John comes over and stands in front of her.)

HULDA
Well—

JOHN
Well—

(There is silly confusion as Hulda hesitates to continue talking about the charivari. She rises and they divert themselves by walking around and examining the furniture, which in reality they know intimately, having chosen it so carefully. John ventures to whistle an air from some ancient tune. He removes his coat. Hulda looks at herself in the mirror of the dresser.)

HULDA
Well—

JOHN
Well—

HULDA
Lizzie Smith made me so mad, I cud'ave kilt her! The very idee! Her givin' me that little, puny canary in a cage as a weddin' present! The idee! And her sayin' that birdie represented *me* and I could be happy like it and sing all the time. That pore little bird!

JOHN
Well— *(He is embarrassed and stammers.)* Ain't you my little honey bird?

HULDA *(changing from her thoughtful attitude)*
Fer the lands sakes, John, do I look like a canary? Don't you see that she was jest tryin' to hurt my feelin's? *(She sniffles and is on the verge of crying.)* I know I'm big, but I don't

34

want no one to be rubbin' it in all the time. I'll git even with her, you jest wait.

JOHN

Aw, fergit it, Huldie. Come an' give me a kiss. (*He goes over near her. Hulda now weeps loudly and convulsively.*) What's the matter?

HULDA

J-J-John, I gotta—Oh, golly, I'm so miserable. I gotta tell you somethin'.

JOHN

Tell me somethin'? Now?

(*He backs away surprised and eyes her with in-increasing wonder and, later, fear, as he drops into a chair.*)

HULDA

Yes, I gotta say it now—and it's gonna make you mad! (*She stops sobbing suddenly and crosses over to John to tower above him as a mighty and violent female, outraged and abused, coming into full consciousness and power for the first time.*) You runt! You sawed-off runt, you! Think you've got me, don't you? Well, you ain't. I ain't your wife, and never will be. I ain't gonna be no canary. I know your trick, you. I know jest the kinda man you are. And my father. And your father. You're all a bunch of cattle-breeders, you are. And women breeders. But you ain't gonna catch *me!* Well, I've fooled all of you. All you slick men. All you tricky Holstein fellers. And all these women gossips. They said I'd never marry—that no man 'ud have me. I've showed 'em. But, Lordie, look what I got!

JOHN (*rising from his chair and trying to placate her, yet keeping at a distance*)
Now, Huldie, now, Huldie—

HULDA (*apparently not paying the least attention to him*)
This is as much *my* farm as it is yourn. Oh, I know how you men got together—I know what Paw promised you. What *you* wanted was this piece of land worth $200 per, *not me.* That's the way every girl around here is kinda auctioned off. Look upon me as a prize head of cattle, don't you? Sorta thrown in with the land. Thought I was gonna be meek and tickled to death to jest get a man, didn't you? Well, I've saw what happened to my Maw and my sister and every woman around here.
You men! You git out in the barnyard and talk Holsteins and wimmen over at the same time. The wonder is, since you gotta association for your cattle, you ain't gotta association for your wimmen. I ain't gonna be no prize breeder!

(*She has reached a declamatory effect, and with the last sentence has come to the center of the stage, where she stands in stark grandeur, arms raised high over her head, fists clenched—an avenging rural goddess. Though we do not appreciate it at first, she commences here an evolutionary process in composure and even in appearance, emerging from yokel awkwardness into a vivacious, passionate, militant Modern; yet she*
36

makes the transformation with such gradual and careful steps that we are hardly aware of definite changes.)

JOHN

Why, Huldie—Why, Huldie—that ain't respectable!

(Hulda still ignores him. She goes over to the bird cage and gazes at the canary.)

HULDA *(tenderly)*

No wonder you're happy, little birdie. You ain't a human bein'. You ain't got all these miseries. Why, you're freer'n me. You ain't gotta worry. There's nothin' to break your heart. You don't have to think and think until you nearly go mad. Folks are kind to you. Just look 'ut us wimmen! Nary one of us is shut up in a cage like yourn—but it's a cage all the same, a bigger, crueler cage—one that kills just as surely. A livin' death! *We* have hearts and brains—we have to think, and we have these awful heart feelin's. *You* can be happy. And I'm gonna make you happier than you've ever bin. I'm gonna let you out—let you go free—you can fly all over everywhere, jest as you please. The idee of folks cagin' up you pretty little birds that God made for outdoors! *(She opens the little cage door and reaches in to bring out the canary. She fondles it and holds it up close to her face. Then she changes her mind and puts it back into the cage.)* No, no, not tonight. I'll let you stay here in your

37

little home 'til mornin'. You might be skeered
o' the dark. But in the mornin', I'll let you
out and you can fly away.

(*John, in the meantime, has been drawing nearer,
his curiosity aroused by her taking the bird out
of the cage. He looks at her grinningly as she pets
the bird, thinking that she has softened, and that
her fit of heroics was merely a bridal nervousness.
He figures that she will quiet down now. He drapes
his arm on her shoulder. She stands motionless.
Then she calmly strides away, leaving his flexed
and suspended arm to flop down ungracefully.*)

JOHN

Now, Huldie, ain't you tired? Ain't you gonna
stop gittin' mad? I ain't mad at what you said.
I fergive you, knowin' as how excitin' it's all bin.
Gee, warn't that a whizz-bang shivaree?
And I betcha Sim is gonna pop the question to
Milly tonight. I jest betcha.

HULDA

Pore Milly! An' I jest betcha she's willin',
the pore fool, to be a slave. But I ain't. Come
here, John. Set down! Let's talk quietly. I ain't
mad. I never was mad at *you* in particular;
it's jest *all* you men. It ain't your fault you're
in the fancy stock business. Your father is.
It sorta runs in this part of Ioway. Now let's
talk.

(*They are seated in two adjoining chairs, rather
stiffly posed. John is in a quandary. It is hardly
his idea of his wedding night. Before he sits*)

38

down, he goes over and turns down the lamp a bit, all in a rather sheepish manner; he draws his chair closer.)

HULDA

Now, John— *(A long pause.)*

JOHN

Well, Huldie—

(A flivver approaches. The motor is turned off. A knock is heard at the door, to their surprise. Both arise; Hulda turns up the lamp. Going to the door, John asks, "Who is there?" He opens the door at the muffled reply. He admits Sim and Milly, both of whom are grinning and simpering and holding hands. Sim is tall, like Hulda. Milly is short, like John. Milly leads Sim over to Hulda and pipes forth in a shrill voice.)

MILLY

He's popped!

(Both Sim and Milly titter. John is embarrassed, not knowing what Hulda will say. But he grins, too. All three watch Hulda, who reverts suddenly to her "company" front.)

HULDA

He's popped? Why, Sim!

JOHN

Hurray!

(Hulda puts her arm around John, much to his surprise, and they enact a lovey-dovey, spoony companionship, such as expected of any Red Bud couple on this momentous occasion. John, en-

39

*couraged, becomes braver and gives her a resound-
ing kiss. And Sim, not to be outdone, does like-
wise with Milly.*)

JOHN

You got a mighty fine gal. An' she's healthy-
like, same as Huldie. Didja ask her during the
shivaree?

SIM

Yes, and she was so tickled. You know, folks
allus said Milly was sorta romantic-like—she's
allus readin' them novels. I don't think it's
good fer a woman to git so many queer idees,
but mebbe until she's married and sorta settled
down, a woman's gotta go through that spell,
jest like a young colt friskin' about.

MILLY

Why, Sim! Comparin' *me* to a colt!

HULDA

Aw, don't mind him, Milly, he didn't mean
nothin'.

MILLY

Well, 'pears to me that he's suddenly awful
serious-like.

SIM

Now that courtship's over, we gotta commence
to think serious-like, ain't we?

MILLY

Oh, Simmie, how can you say that. I ain't
been engaged but a hour!

(*Milly is rather put out and inclined to pout. She
goes over to Hulda, while John and Sim edge off
toward the kitchen.*)

40

JOHN (*addressing Sim*)
I got somethin' to show you, Sim.

(*Winks at Sim, indicates the flask in his pocket, and ushers him out. Milly gives a furtive glance at the disappearing men, and comes over close to Hulda and asks in a hushed voice.*)

MILLY
Skairt?

HULDA
No—are you?

(*Hulda says the "No" with an air of defiance, as Milly glances at the kitchen door. The "Are you?" comes with less feeling.*)

MILLY
No, seein' as you're not. 'Course, it ain't *my* weddin' night—like yourn. But I remember how skeered Mame was on her weddin' night. Most girls are, ain't they? And do you remember Grace Brown, how queer-like she acted, fer days and days?

HULDA
Well, Milly, don't you be feared, now. (*As to herself, in a vehement manner.*) It ain't right fer men to skeer women that way.

MILLY
Why, Huldie, how you talk!

HULDA
Oh, don't pay any attention to me. Be skeered, if you wanta. It'd be more natural—most wimmen like to be sorta skairdish—that's why Sim compared you to a colt.

MILLY (*in a confidential tone*)

Huldie, I wouldn't talk about bein' skeered, but I walked under a ladder this very mornin', and you know what bad luck that is. I jest made up my mind this mornin' that Sim would never ask me, and I'd be an old maid. I jest worried and worried all day. You know as how Jim Fuller died, right after walkin' under a ladder. I tell you, Huldie, it's a bad sign! Jest as bad as meetin' a funeral.

HULDA

No worse'n hearin' bells toll all the time in your head, when there ain't no bells ringin'.

MILLY

I never heared of that. Is it such a bad sign? And who's ever heared 'em? (*She notes Hulda's nervousness.*) Not *you*, Hulda?

(*Before Hulda can answer, John and Sim enter from the kitchen, as Sim hands a flask back to John, who puts it in his pocket. Both smack their lips. They are laughing and talking as they enter.*)

JOHN

Sure, I'm gonna go to the sale tomorrow. I want two more draught mares.

SIM

Stop by for me, won't you, John?

JOHN

Yes, I'll be passin' by about ten.

(*Sim goes over to Milly and flippantly chucks her under the chin.*)

42

SIM (*to Milly*)

Ain't mad, are you?

MILLY

Now, Sim, don't keep carrin' on. 'Course I ain't mad. Not on sech a night as this. A girl ain't engaged but onct.

HULDA (*sharply*)

Not hereabouts, at least.

JOHN

Now, Huldie—

SIM

Gee, Hulda, you're sharp with your tongue. You're allus puttin' ideas in people's minds. I'd jest like to ast you if girls get engaged and unengaged, time and time agin, in other parts. I think that 'ud be wicked—keepin' men guessin' all the time. I think a feller'd oughta know, else how's he gonna be sure of a woman as 'ud stick by him?

MILLY

Now don't *you* git mad. 'Pears to me we're actin' sorta strange-like tonight, gettin' in all these arguments. (*She soothes Sim, caressing him and leading him to a chair and getting him to sit down.*) Now, let's all talk nice. Let's talk about marriage!

HULDA

Let's talk about somethin' else.

MILLY

Why? Why not? (*To John.*) *You* want, don't you, John?

JOHN

No. What's there to talk about marriage?

Hulda and me is hitched—now it's up to Sim and you. The less talkin' about it, 'pears to me, the better. I say (*addressing Sim*), let the wimmen-folks talk about marriage 'mong theirselves—but even that takes time away from their work. It ain't a decent subject to talk about, jest among folks, as though one was talkin' about the weather, er crops, er cattle, er the county fair, er ottamobiles, er the Scripture.

SIM

That's the way I feel about it, too, John. Wimmen, as are busy, ain't got time fer all that sorta talk about marriage. Anyhow, it's between a man and his wife—nobody else.

(*Milly is assenting to this talk, taking it meekly, as is the custom among her kind, but Hulda, sitting at the back of the group, shows defiant disgust at such preachment.*)

MILLY

Now, you're serious again. I don't know what's come over us—we were havin' sech a good time durin' the shivaree—an' now we git so serious-like every time we start to talk.

HULDA

Well, wouldn't you like somethin' to eat? I think there's some cake in the kitchen. Shall I git some?

SIM

Oh, no, we can't stay. We jest snuck back from the shivareers, seein' the light still burnin'. And thinkin' you'd wanta know.

44

(*But they suddenly forget Hulda and John and commence to spoon in rural ardor. Whenever they glance at John and Hulda, they find the latter indulging in the same fervid pastime. But when they are not looking, Hulda sits stiff as a statue.*)

MILLY (*as Sim gives her such a squeeze of violence that she gasps and chokes*)
Why, Sim! Sim*mie*!

(*This creates such a commotion that she rises and gives him a playful slap and then rushes to the door, as he flutters after her. They stop at the door and grin and inspect the nuptial chamber meaningly. Milly runs to Hulda and surprises her with a kiss. Sim fishes out a baby's rattle from his pocket and gives it to John with a hearty slap on the back and a loud guffaw. Then Milly and Sim leave. Hulda pushes John away with vigor and stalks around the room, lioness-like.*)

HULDA
She's jest a plumb damn fool—and there's millions like her. Lettin' some man, jest because he *is* a man, fool her into thinkin' she's won a prize. Wish't I'd had the nerve to tell her to go onna strike! Like as I am. If all us farm wimmen got together and organized, we'd make men-folks treat us decent. The idee! No woman orta have twelve children. Those city wimmen are right. Men can't fool *them*. Men jest eat outa their hands. But around here, it's jest t'other way. (*She goes over to John, who has sunk down in a chair from ex-*

*haustion and surprise at this new onslaught.
She shakes her fist in the face of this apparently
harmless little man.)* You brute! (*He makes a move
of withdrawal and shrinkage from this furious
female, while she stalks back and forth with clenched
fists and in fighting attitude. He slips out the
flask of booze from his pocket and takes a big
gulp. This he repeats during the next few minutes,
as opportunity presents itself.*) The time's comin'
when men like you and Sim and the rest are all
gonna meet yer equals—marriage ain't gonna
be so lop-sided. Farm wimmen ain't gonna be
dumb animals no more'n city wimmen.

JOHN

Now, Huldie, I can't stand all this—you're goin'
too fer—what's come over you so suddent. I
never knew you had sech spells. I—

HULDA

You shut up, you! *I'm* gonna do the talkin'.
You done all the taffyin' you're ever gonna do
with me. *I'm* gonna boss this shebang. You
watch me. I—

JOHN (*timidly*)

You're *not!*

HULDA (*furiously*)

I *am!*

JOHN

Ain't *I* your lawful husband? Didn't you
promise during the ceremony to *obey?* You
act as if you don't know a wife's duties. You
ain't meek.

HULDA

Obey? Meek? Obey *you?* 'Course I'm not—

ain't I makin' it clear? Then I'll say it agin:
I'm gonna be the boss of this farm—you've done
all the bossin' you'll ever do with *me*. I'm
boss *now*.

JOHN (*more bravely*)
You're *not!*

HULDA
I *am!* (*With final decision, as if closing the subject.*)

JOHN
Then I'll leave you. I ain't gonna be run by
no woman, by God!

HULDA
Then git out, if you wanta. The sooner, the
better. I guess I can run this farm, without the
like o' *you*.

JOHN (*oratorically*)
But what'll people say? (*This strikes Hulda at
first as a terrible blow. She falters in her militant
striding—she looks at him horror-stricken. And,
triumphantly, he notes the effect. His liquor has
made him braver, more loquacious. Hulda sinks in
a chair.*) Yes, what'll people say? If I up and
leaves you on our bridal night? What'll folks
think about you—what 'ud *you* think of a bride
whose man up and left her sorta mysterious-like
—never sayin' a word. For I'd never tell what's
wrong with you. I'd never tell about this here
spell of yourn. Whatta you think people'd say
about you?

HULDA
I know. All the mean, lyin' people. I know.
And *you* know.

47

JOHN

Well, they wouldn't blame *me*.

HULDA

No, *you'd* be a hero. I'd be the prize leper around here—this here farm'd be a leper's island—no one would come near me. The union of mothers would be agin me. The union of Holstein breeders would be agin me. I'd be called crazy. And I tell you it's all wrong— all wrong. It's slavery. I'm caged in a prison of gossiping tongues—shootin' out at me like poison snakes

JOHN

Now you're talkin' sense. You'd better think of what folks'd say. Some 'ud think you had a pheezical disease. You know what folks say.

(*Hulda rises and throws off the pall of this situation—regaining control.*)

HULDA

Well, I don't care. I don't give a dern what folks say—all the people in this country—all the people in the world. Or the minister. You can't skeer me no more, John. Fer a minnut, you nearly got me—but, pshaw, let gossips talk. Tongues wag anyhow.

JOHN

You mean you don't care what folks say about you or *me?*

HULDA (*decisively*)

No!

(John recognizes the sudden turn against him. The liquor has given him courage.)

JOHN

Then, by God, I'll tame you another way! *(He takes a revolver from a bureau drawer and goes over to Hulda and places it at her head. She does not move an inch—but stands like a martyr, ready for execution.)* Now, we'll have an end to this craziness. You damned trouble-maker, you—you—I'll show you who's boss here. All you're gabbin's gotta stop. All your suffragittin.'

HULDA *(soothingly)*

Now, John—

JOHN

Shut up! I ain't foolin'.

HULDA

I *was.* That was all put on.

(John relaxes from his melodramatic posture. She becomes kittenish and appealing, a farm siren.)

JOHN

Then you never meant none of it?

HULDA

Nope, was jest foolin'. I didn't know what else to do. I'm jest so embarrassed.

JOHN

And you'll love and obey me?

HULDA

Sure. I think you're grand.

JOHN

Then let's fergit it all. Let's make up. Come, give me a kiss.

(*They apparently make up with great gusto. During the embrace Hulda sniffs as though she had just detected the alcoholic perfume, and feels the flask, as if she had discovered it for the first time.*)

HULDA

What's that? Whiskey? Go on—have some more. Ain't you been havin' some all evenin'? Let me have a drop. I'm so tired—jest plumb done up.

(*John takes a big swig. He shows that his earlier drinks have had their effect. Hulda makes believe at imbibing. She urges him to take more. He becomes very maudlin, hanging on to Hulda. Strangely enough he still carries the revolver, bandying it in his limp hand. During the gyrations of affection, it suddenly goes off, at a harmless angle. Hulda faints in his arms and sinks to the floor—a vast human lump, flat on her back. John takes a big drink, then another. He is thoroughly drunk.*)

JOHN

Oh, my God, I've gone and killed her! (*He stoops down and lays his head on her breast and weeps in inebriated alarm.*) My poor little Huldie! (*He feels her heart—her chest—to be certain that she is really dead.*) She's dead! (*He works her arms up and down, as though she had been drowned.*) God, what a loss! Jest like the time that bull died on me. Oh, what kin I do? Who can I marry now? Now—I'll be hanged fer killin' her! I might jest as well die, too. (*He lies down beside her, resting his head carefully on her outstretched arm. He lets the pistol thump to the floor. He wipes the tears from his face. He shuts his eyes.*)

(*A bell tolls far off—so faintly that one barely catches its sound. Hulda recovers slowly from her faint, then sits up suddenly. John's head slides to the floor; he is dead drunk. Hulda looks at him pityingly—the nasty thing—she edges away from him quietly. She crawls over to the dresser—takes out an everyday dress. She removes her wedding dress, laying it lengthwise on one side of the bed. She puts on her everyday dress. All the time she eyes John in his drunken and snoring slumber. When preparations for departure are complete, she goes over and drags him to the bed—lifts him onto it—beside the wedding dress. Then she goes quickly to the door, ready to escape, giving John a final glance. Exultant in her freedom, she opens the door—but suddenly runs back across the room, snatches the bird cage with the surprised occupant—and rushes out.*)

(CURTAIN)

MISS MYRTLE SAYS "YES"

PERSONS IN THE PLAY

MISS MYRTLE, *the Village Milliner*
PANSY, *her Younger Sister*
MRS. UPJOHN, *a Gossip*
MR. FISHBACK, *a Farmer*

MISS MYRTLE SAYS "YES" was presented for the first time
at the Cameo Theatre, Chicago, February 23, 1922.

MISS MYRTLE SAYS "YES"

It is always a particularly trying time in any millinery shop just before the "Easter Opening." The stock gets so low. Only the unpopular hats remain, pathetic mementos of rejection. Everything seems so dreary. There is always a lull in business while everyone waits for the new styles.

The Bon Ton in Red Bud was going through this annual period of depression—the Easter crates had not even arrived yet. Miss Pansy, who with her sister, is the arbiter of Red Bud fashion, always thrills at the coming of the crates and revels in opening them.

As she stands there beside a table, listening intently to Mrs. Upjohn, a faithful customer, who pauses at the door, one imagines that Miss Pansy is very anxious to enliven the drab table displays with the fresher offerings which will arrive soon.

Winter still lingers in Red Bud, but spring has not been delayed in Pansy's heart. This is evidenced by her costume. Although her old, brown serge skirt is reminiscent of the passing season, she has on a new waist. It is decorated with much cheap lace. Her toilette is accented further by a necklace of gaudy glass beads. She has just read in a fashion journal that beads are the vogue.

The wall-cases are as uninteresting as the table displays. Even the window trim proclaims that neither of the sisters has bestowed much attention upon it for several weeks.

Miss Pansy realizes that a "spring cleaning" is due. It always precedes the coming of the Easter shipment. The bell over the door, which tinkles the arrival of a customer, is so very dusty. And the furniture needs polishing.

It would not be a bad idea to have the walls papered, if it doesn't cost too much. The rear wall, particularly, needs attention—over the door leading to the rear workroom the paper has been peeling off all winter.

Miss Pansy has been itemizing mentally the routine of "spring cleaning" while listening to Mrs. Upjohn, who glances from Pansy to the street, intent both on interesting Pansy with the latest gossip and keeping an eye on the passers-by.

Mrs. Upjohn is the village gossip. She is here on one of her frequent visits, dispensing and gathering the latest "grape-vine" news. She is tall and gaunt—kittenish, however, and ever attempting to maintain her girlish charm.

One must listen to Mrs. Upjohn, for she gives forth daily what the "Star" never dares to print, even weekly. She is ably assisted as a sort of later-day town-crier by her husband, Will Upjohn, the proprietor of The Elite Tonsorial Parlor, which is just down the street from The Bon Ton.

Mrs. Upjohn is on her way there now with the daily supply of fresh towels—a journey that permits of many way-stations, for she goes down one street, then around the square, then home by another street.

As she hovers near the door, one realizes that she is paying more attention to Pansy than usual and less to the events of the street.

She has long been expecting something romantic of Pansy, who, now thirty and on the verge of spinsterhood, has so far provided no juicy tidbit, for this village newsmonger.

"Those Clark sisters," Mrs. Upjohn would say, "certainly orta get married," and while women would agree with her sympathetically, no man seemed to be interested.

Miss Myrtle, of course, was really not considered any longer, having sunk into the touch-me-not category of "old maid," but Miss Pansy had long been a candidate for a match. Mrs. Upjohn had hoped that Fred Snellenberger could be interested, and Miss Pansy had been invited to several "socials" by the Upjohns, in the hope that Fred could be paired off with Pansy—but somehow or other nothing ever came of it.

On this particular morning, Mrs. Upjohn has been relating a strange story to Miss Pansy, who apparently would rather not hear it.

MRS. UPJOHN (*confidentially, while Miss Pansy listens tensely*)

. . . and the sexton saw a light out in the cemetery—it was jest after dark, and he went out there to the Pierson's lot and he nearly caught 'em right there. The man musta bin smokin'. That gave them away. The sexton wasn't quick enough—he couldn't tell exactly *who* they were. (*Miss Pansy relaxes her tensity, though it is quickly roused again.)* But folks sorta have an idea who the couple was.

(*Looking closely at Miss Pansy, as if expecting to find a sign of guilt.*)

MISS PANSY (*with nervous nonchalance*)
Well, there ain't no park in Red Bud.

MRS. UPJOHN (*tartly*)
That don't make it right.

MISS PANSY
A girl as works at the hotel, waitin' on tables, ain't got no place to take her beau, except to the cemetery or the deppo.

MRS. UPJOHN
Who said it was a girl from the hotel?

MISS PANSY
Well, I was just guessin'. Seems like waitin' on table's the *only* way to meet a *man*—here in Red Bud.

MRS. UPJOHN (*horrified*)
But *drummers?* Most of 'em ain't nice. Mr. Upjohn says—

MISS PANSY
I'd *make* 'em nice.

MRS. UPJOHN
Well, I don't know what things are comin' to. Seems to me the young folks are jest broke loose. Have you heard about that Burber girl and that travelin' man? They say she was gonna elope with him, but her mother found it out and sicked the Jedge on her darter—you know Mrs. Burber works at the Jedge's—and he druv the travelin' man out of town. And it

got all around—you know how people will gossip—I tell you drummers are terrible men. Everything is terrible nowadays. Why, t'other night Mr. Upjohn and me went to the movies and I saw one of them vampires squirming around—oh, it was positively awful—I think them pitchers oughtn't be shown. Think of the example! Some of the boys put their arms right on the backs of the girl's seats, right there at the theatre, something terrible. I jest felt *so* embarrassed. Why, when I was a little younger, if a young man went so far as that— well, I tell you things are jest gittin' worse and worse. Now I—

MISS PANSY

Don't you jest love the movies?

MRS. UPJOHN

Yes, but I tell you them actors and actresses live terrible lives. Why, I read in the papers about one actress that—
But we're gittin' off'n the subject. (*With searching directness.*) Where was *you* on the night of that cemetery affair? (*Miss Pansy is startled and embarrassed.*)

(*The door from the rear room opens. Miss Myrtle enters. She is considerably older than her sister—in fact, she is forty, which is very old in Red Bud for a "maiden lady." She is thin, a frail icicle—tall, spare, and angular. Her features are sharp and her face has lost what kindliness it may have once possessed. Her expres-*

*sion is acid. Her voice is nasal, chill, and stac-
cato.*

*Of late years Miss Myrtle has retired to the
workroom almost completely, leaving Miss Pansy
to deal with the customers. Also, Miss Myrtle
has been burdened with the financial responsi-
bilities of the little establishment, finding it in-
creasingly difficult each year to make ends meet.
Her hair is gray and thin. Her costume is an
ancient wool dress of simple and nondescript cut.
She carries a hat which she has been working on
and deposits it on a table.)*

MRS. UPJOHN

Howdy, Miss Myrtle.

MISS MYRTLE

How'd do, Mrs. Upjohn.

MRS. UPJOHN

I was just tellin' your sister I must run along.
I jest dropped in to ask when the spring
things are comin' in. Easter openin' purty
soon?

MISS MYRTLE

Well, any time now. Yes, soon. I expect a
shipment this week.

*(She takes up a hat and looks it over, then car-
ries it to the rear room.)*

MRS. UPJOHN

As I was sayin', *you* mustn't keep puttin' off
gittin' married. You're thirty, now, ain't you!
I tell you, I'd rather be *Mrs.* Upjohn, even if
he is sorta rheumatic, than be called an *old*

60

maid! Now, Pansy, you mustn't wait like your sister. You're too pretty. Jest make your mind up *not* to be an old maid, and the man will come along. You orta land a good man—say, don't these millinery drummers sorta shine up to you? I know there ain't many men here in Red Bud. And most of them are lookin' for regular farm hands. But you jest get busy—find your man. (*Confidentially.*) Ain't I seen you talkin' to Mr. Fishback?

MISS PANSY (*frightened, lest her sister hear*)
Ss-s-sh, be careful!

MRS. UPJOHN
Well, he's not to be sneezed at, even if he is a widower. I can remember the day when your sister thought he was purty nice. If you can hook him—I say, do it. It's better'n waitin' and waitin'. A bird in the hand is worth two in the bush, you know. And if you don't want to have folks allus sorta wonderin' if you're gonna be an old maid like your sister, I say, sorta edge up to him.

MISS PANSY
Please let's not talk about it now—with my sister in the next room. Some other time. Please not now.

MRS. UPJOHN
Well, she oughtn't to be jealous. She oughtn't to stand in your way. 'Pears to me, she's always been skeerin' your men off.

(*Miss Myrtle enters.*)

MRS. UPJOHN
Well, I really *must* go. What you say about
the new styles is most interestin', Miss Pansy.
I'll be in to your spring openin'. (*She bustles
towards the door.*) Good-bye.

MISS MYRTLE
Good-bye.

MISS PANSY (*who acts frightened and as if she
must talk further with Mrs. Upjohn*)
Oh, wait, Mrs. Upjohn, I'll walk up your way.
I have to go to the post-office to get our mail.
Wait just a minute. (*She puts on her things
quickly, while Mrs. Upjohn lingers at the door.*)
Anything fer me to git, Myrtle?

MISS MYRTLE
No, nothin' I can think of.

MISS PANSY
I'll be right back.

(*She and* Mrs. *Upjohn leave.*)

MISS MYRTLE
What a miserable old trouble-maker. I wish
she'd leave Pansy alone.

(*She sits down, sewing on a hat. She hums "Old
Hundred." The clock strikes a slow and monoton-
ous twelve.
Enter Mr. Fishback, dressed in his Sunday-best.
He is a ruddy, well-built man, not as old at forty
as many farmers. He is in apologetic, hesitant
mood. Miss Myrtle looks up with surprise.*)

Mr. Fishback!

62

MR. FISHBACK
They sent me *here*.

MISS MYRTLE
They?

MR. FISHBACK
Yes, the bank.

MISS MYRTLE
Well?

MR. FISHBACK
They said you—you had bought the mortgage.

MISS MYRTLE
Well, what of it?

MR. FISHBACK
Yes, but—

MISS MYRTLE
Ain't a person got a right to make an investment?

MR. FISHBACK
But the mortgage on *my* farm.

MISS MYRTLE
Same as any to me.

MR. FISHBACK
Now, Myrtle—

MISS MYRTLE
Don't "Myrtle" me. That day's passed years ago.

MR. FISHBACK
Then you did it to get even?

MISS MYRTLE
No, six per cent.

MR. FISHBACK (*unctuously*)
Did you do it because of old-times' sakes?

MISS MYRTLE

I said "six per cent."

MR. FISHBACK

Well, I can't take it up. I know it's due. But
I can't take it up. That's why I went to the
bank to-day.

MISS MYRTLE

What's that got to do with me?

MR. FISHBACK

You'd not foreclose?

MISS MYRTLE

Yes.

MR. FISHBACK

You'd drive me and the children off'n the farm?
Where I've worked all these years? Jest be-
cause I can't meet the payment? That ain't
Christianlike.

MISS MYRTLE (*fiercely*)

The likes of *you* needn't be tellin' *me* what's
Christianlike.

MR. FISHBACK (*meekly*)

I didn't mean nothin'. But I thought you
wouldn't be so hard. Can't old times sorta
soften you?

MISS MYRTLE

You know the day I became a hard woman.
And I've never softened up yet—and never will.
You ditched me. Now take the consequences.
And don't be whinin' around here. Customers
is likely to come in. Besides, I've made up my
mind. It's purely a business proposition. I'm
too old for sentiment. I'm a good deal older

64

—and you know it—than when we were—
engaged.

MR. FISHBACK

You ain't hated me all these years?

MISS MYRTLE

I have.

MR. FISHBACK

You ain't sorry for me, now I have had all this
trouble—my wife dyin', crops poor, money
scarce?

MISS MYRTLE

Not a bit.

MR. FISHBACK

My, you're hard.

MISS MYRTLE

Harder than you know.

MR. FISHBACK

Do you mean you've been slavin' and savin'
all these years jest to git even with me?

MISS MYRTLE

Think what you please.

MR. FISHBACK

You act as though I ruined your life.

MISS MYRTLE

Well, you came very near—

MR. FISHBACK

Why, I—

MISS MYRTLE

I thought you had for a while—but I saw you
ruin another woman's life.

MR. FISHBACK

You mean you hate me—not because I didn't
marry *you*—but jest on general principles?

MISS MYRTLE

That's it. I think you're a—

MR. FISHBACK

You mean you'd take it out on me just out of pity for the woman I married instead of you? I don't believe that.

MISS MYRTLE

Oh, let's stop talkin'. It does no good. I don't care what you think. I don't care to tell you what I think. You came on business—

MR. FISHBACK

Well, I can't pay the mortgage.

MISS MYRTLE

Then we're through.

MR. FISHBACK

Do you mean it?

MISS MYRTLE

Certainly.

MR. FISHBACK

I must get the money, or you'll foreclose?

MISS MYRTLE

Yes.

MR. FISHBACK

But I can't get the money.

MISS MYRTLE

That's your affair.

MR. FISHBACK

But what will become of me and the children?

MISS MYRTLE

That doesn't worry *me*.

MR. FISHBACK

My, but you're a hard woman.

MISS MYRTLE

You're repeatin' yourself. You'd better be
spendin' the time rustlin' the money.

MR. FISHBACK

You'll be sorry.

MISS MYRTLE

Don't you think it. I don't know what it
is to be sorry. You can't do anything to hurt
me—I've got you where I want you.

MR. FISHBACK

Now, Myrtle—if we could talk *everything* over

MISS MYRTLE

Good-day, Mr. Fishback.

(*He sees the helplessness of the situation and
leaves, whipped.*)

MISS MYRTLE (*to herself.*)

Ugh, I'm glad that's over.

(*She sits and sews, rocking and humming. The
whole monotony of her life is typified here for
a moment or two, in a longer than usual tableau.
It makes even the audience fidget at such futility.
Enter Miss Pansy. She removes her coat and hat
and bustles around the room, collecting things to
work upon.*)

MISS PANSY

I must get that hat ready for the Baumgart
funeral to-morrow. Where is the crape? (*She
pulls it out of a box.*) Oh, here it is. (*Looking
at her sister curiously.*) What makes you so
quiet to-day, Myrtle? You hardly spoke to
Mrs. Upjohn.

MISS MYRTLE (*tartly*)
Busy people ain't got time to gas.

(*Miss Pansy sits in a rocker, too, and both rock back and forth, Miss Myrtle slowly, Miss Pansy jerkily.*)

MISS PANSY
Well, you needn't think I enjoy this gloom every day. Sometimes I feel like screaming. Your rocking and humming makes me nervous. And when spring comes, I feel all cooped up. (*Meditatively and to herself.*) I must get away!

MISS MYRTLE (*startled*)
Get away? What's Mrs. Upjohn been putting in your head. What do you mean, Pansy?

MISS PANSY (*surprised at having said out loud what she had been saying so constantly to herself*)
Well, I might as well tell you I'm getting desperate. I ain't going on here making hats for life. I hate hats. I hate all this skimping—living like we're waiting only to die. I'd think *you'd* go crazy.

MISS MYRTLE
Why, Pansy, what's come over you? You've been actin' lately as if you ain't feelin' well. Mebbe you'd better lay down for a spell.

MISS PANSY
No, I ain't sick like you think. It's another kind of sickness.

(*There is a pause, and the continuous, but slower, rocking.*)

68

MISS PANSY (*impatiently.*)

Oh! Myrtle, I don't want to argue again and go over the thing that's always stood between us—but I can't go on—I can't stand this. (*Indicating the room.*) I want to live like other women—*I want to get married!*

(*She throws down her work and walks around the shop.*)

MISS MYRTLE (*rather sneeringly*)

Pooh. You want trouble!

MISS PANSY

Well, then, I want trouble. Anything—anything—anything but this, this— (*She is inarticulate in gesturing her loathing of the scene.*)

MISS MYRTLE

Well, you're old enough to know what you want, yet you're a fool.

MISS PANSY

Then I want to be a bigger fool. I want to be the kind of a great big fool every married woman is.

MISS MYRTLE

Where's any man around here you're gonna get?

MISS PANSY

He's *here*, or he's somewhere.

MISS MYRTLE

You gonna start out and find him? Where's the money coming from for all that gallivantin'?

MISS PANSY

I don't know. But I know I'd rather be a bad woman than an old maid.

MISS MYRTLE

That's insulting *me*.

MISS PANSY

I don't mean it that way. But I don't care. I'm not going to be an old maid, and I think your life is a failure. So there. That's said. The trouble with us is that we never talk right out—you seem afraid to let yourself go. You act so hard.

MISS MYRTLE (*startled by the word*)

Hard? A hard woman?

MISS PANSY

Well, you know what I think now. Ain't you going to help me, or are you going to be hard with me, and hinder me, as you always have?

MISS MYRTLE

No, I cannot help you, or any woman, find a man. I hate men. I have found my salvation in being single. I will never marry. And I tell you, you are looking for trouble.

MISS PANSY

You mean to deny me *my* kind of happiness because of your own experience. You're selfish. For years you've kept me like a prisoner. (*Miss Pansy stops in front of her sister, who looks up at her defiantly.*) Well, I am going to tell you everything—and right now. We might as well have it out once and for all. You and I are different, and you can't make *me* an old maid —never. I am going to marry Mr. Fishback!

(*Miss Myrtle rises, overcome with surprise. She seizes her sister by the shoulders, looking her squarely in the face.*)

MISS MYRTLE

No! Never! Never Fishback! Never *that* man!

MISS PANSY

Let go. You're hurting me.

MISS MYRTLE

You can't marry *him!*

MISS PANSY

Can't? Why not? You'd say that about *any* man, I suppose. It's part of your game, is it?

MISS MYRTLE

He's a widower.

MISS PANSY

He's the man I've looked for—my man.

MISS MYRTLE

He's no man.

MISS PANSY

What is he?

MISS MYRTLE

He—he—he is a murderer!

MISS PANSY

A murderer! (*Her first surprise ebbs as she thinks it is a mere bluff to dissuade her.*) Oh, that's part of your game. I believe you'd go any lengths to keep me an old maid. Who'd *he* ever kill?

MISS MYRTLE

Me.

MISS PANSY

You? What do you mean?

MISS MYRTLE
He's the man that made me a hard woman.

MISS PANSY
I don't understand.

MISS MYRTLE
We was engaged—years ago. He left me in the lurch, marrying that Eckhart girl, because her folks had land.

MISS PANSY
You were engaged?

MISS MYRTLE (*looking away, embarrassed*)
Yes—he was my—my lover.

MISS PANSY (*sympathetically*)
O, Myrtle!

(*It is evidently a blow, but she conceals it from her sister.*)

MISS MYRTLE
You know now. And you know the kind of a life his wife led—he drove her to the grave. But I don't hate him for that. I hate him for what he did to *me*.

MISS PANSY
Then you didn't want to be an old maid?

MISS MYRTLE (*vigorously*)
No, I didn't. What woman— (*Catches herself in time and freezes up.*) I learned my lesson. All men are mean. And Carl Fishback is meaner than the meanest. He spoilt my life. But I figger I am better off.
(*A pause, as they think over the situation.*)
I guess that cooks his goose with you, don't

it. You'd never marry him *now*, would you?
A man as ruined your sister.

MISS PANSY (*slowly and deliberately*)

I don't care. I can't judge you and him. I
don't know all that happened. I've got my own
life to live. I've freed myself from you, now.
(*She walks about restlessly.*)
Yes, I'll marry him anyways!

MISS MYRTLE

Pansy!

MISS PANSY

I want him. At first, I didn't care *what man*.
Any man, so as to escape all this. Then, when
I got to know Mr. Fishback I was glad—and
I'm going to marry him. I don't care if people
say he's no good—every woman wants her man,
and *I* think he *is* good. But even if he *wasn't*,
I'd marry him.

MISS MYRTLE

Why, that's wicked.

MISS PANSY

Well, I may be a wicked woman. I don't
know. But I do know I'm lonesome. And you
and I have never got along very well. You've
skairt away every beau I ever had. So I just
made up my mind—

MISS MYRTLE

Why, what do you mean?

MISS PANSY

This: As a wife, with my children and my husband, my family, my home—I'd rather fight
and scrap, and make up, and go through
troubles, than look forward to sewing and sewing

73

and sewing. I'm old enough to know that marriage ain't heaven on earth, but this store is worse—it's just like a penitentiary.

MISS MYRTLE

You hate me?

MISS PANSY

No, I don't hate you, but—but—I wasn't made to live with a woman.

MISS MYRTLE

You'd break off with me forever, just to marry that Fishback?

MISS PANSY

If that's your price.

MISS MYRTLE

Well, *he* can't marry you.

MISS PANSY (*in fresh surprise*)

First you say *I* can't marry him. Now you say *he* can't marry me. Why not?

MISS MYRTLE

He's broke. Ain't got a cent. In debt. And two children. And he's over forty.

MISS PANSY

Well, if he ain't a good farmer, he's a pretty good handy man and he can work for wages.

MISS MYRTLE

Work? He's no worker. That's why he's taken up auctioneering on the side. He's *all* mouth.

MISS PANSY

I wouldn't care if he was a day laborer, working on the tracks. I wouldn't care if he was a dago in a box car. We've been goin' together on the quiet—we've an understanding, and I've said

74

"Yes." I won't wait until I lose my chance.
And it's too late now for you to stop us—we
kept it a secret. I was afraid of *you*. But I
ain't now.

MISS MYRTLE

You're engaged!

MISS PANSY

He—we have an understanding.

MISS MYRTLE

Why, his wife's not been dead a year!

MISS PANSY

Well?

MISS MYRTLE

But what'll people say?

MISS PANSY

I don't care. The married women will understand, and the old maids will be jealous. You
might as well give into it, Myrtle.

MISS MYRTLE

You'll have to support him, I bet.

MISS PANSY

What if I do? Won't be any harder than the
work I'm doing now. Anyway, how do you
know he won't work? *You* try to make him out
the very worst. I like him. Folks like him.
He's popular. You're the only one that hates
him. He's jolly and always happy. He's kind.
He may have made a mistake in turning you
down—but we all make mistakes. You should
have got another man. You can't blame Carl
Fishback altogether.

MISS MYRTLE

Well, the next woman he marries will either

75

run *him* or he'll run *her* into an early grave.
You ain't the one to conquer him. He'd make
life miserable for you.

MISS PANSY

I'm willing to take the chance.

(*Miss Myrtle gets up from her chair suddenly
as if an inspiration had flashed across her mind.
She makes a gesture of determination—unseen
by Pansy—and shows plainly that she is going
to take the situation into her own hands.*)

MISS MYRTLE

We won't talk about it any more. We'll think
it over. I'll tell you some more about him—
after while.

MISS PANSY

It is no use. I've made up my mind. It is
all settled.

(*Miss Myrtle is putting on her cloak and hat.*)

MISS MYRTLE

We will talk about it later. I must traipse
over to the bank now, before the cashier goes
to dinner. (*Miss Myrtle goes out. The door
has hardly slammed, when she comes back, holds
it open for a moment, and says dramatically*)
There's one thing for you to think over—and
that is: You'll never marry Carl Fishback!
(*Then she departs.*)

(*Miss Pansy shrugs her shoulders, does not answer, but picks up her work and sews for a minute. "I will, I must," she says with determina-*

tion to the absent Myrtle. Then she leans back in her chair in contemplative mood. The silence is complete. Enter Mrs. Upjohn, cautiously, so quietly that Miss Pansy does not hear her at first, but is startled by the voice.)

MRS. UPJOHN (*excited and out of breath*)
Why, why your sister walked right out of here, right down to the corner—and—and she's *talking* to Mr. Fishback!

MISS PANSY
She is! (*She jumps out of her chair and goes to the door.*)

MRS. UPJOHN
The first time in *years!*

MISS PANSY
Where?

MRS. UPJOHN
Right there at the corner. (*She gets her breath.*) Right in front of the bank. Where he was standing. People are just staring at them. I couldn't get here fast enough to tell you. I knew *you'd* want to know.

MISS PANSY
I?

MRS. UPJOHN (*kittenishly*)
Now, don't put on so. Folks are talking about you and him. You're not so foxy.

MISS PANSY
Talking about us?

MRS. UPJOHN
Yes, and I suppose he's asking Miss Myrtle to say "yes" to your marrying him.

7

MISS PANSY

Why, Mrs. Upjohn!

MRS. UPJOHN

Well, he'd have to make up to her, wouldn't he—and sorta smooth things over, if you and him was married. You know they ain't spoke for nearly twenty years, and everybody knows it. And there they are, standing right out in front of everybody, talking quiet-like, jest as if they were friends. They were so puzzlin', though. *I* couldn't tell whether they were making up or quarreling. I jest wonder. (*Point blank.*) Are you and him engaged?

MISS PANSY

Well—no.

MRS. UPJOHN

Folks say so. But what about the mortgage?

MISS PANSY (*in astonishment*)

The mortgage!

MRS. UPJOHN

Yes. Your sister jest about owns everything of his'n. Didn't you know that?

MISS PANSY

No.

MRS. UPJOHN (*in surprise*)

Oh! Fer land's sakes. (*Then nodding knowingly.*) I see. Then your sister never knew that you and him was goin' together?

MISS PANSY

She knows now.

MRS. UPJOHN (*knowingly, as if she were piecing facts together*)

I see. So that's how the land lays. (*She*

fidgets around, goes to the door, holds it open as she looks up the street.) I'll see if they are still standing there. Yes, still talking. No, now they're leaving!—together!—coming this way—why, I believe they're coming *here*! I must be goin'. They *are* coming here! What do you think of that. Him and her walkin' down Main Street. And coming here. She's likely said "Yes" to your marryin' him. And they're made up. I'll bet *you're* glad. I must go. (*She bustles out.*)

(*Miss Pansy is in a quandary. She flurries about the room in consternation, not knowing what to do. Then she hurries to the back room, closing the door.*)

(*Enter Miss Myrtle, followed by Mr. Fishback. They look about carefully, particularly at the door to the rear room. Miss Myrtle is mistress of the situation. Mr. Fishback is crushed and meek.*)

MISS MYRTLE
　　She's not here. She's gone out to get lunch ready.

MR. FISHBACK
　　But what'll we say to her?

MISS MYRTLE
　　Well, you'd better let me do most of the talkin'. I can't trust you.

MR. FISHBACK
　　But—won't you listen—I must tell you　—

MISS MYRTLE
　　You ain't set no weddin' date?

MR. FISHBACK
No, but—

MISS MYRTLE (*constantly interrupting him*)
Talk fast—she may come in.

MR. FISHBACK
But we got a sorta understanding. (*Hopelessly.*) I didn't know I was gonna get in such a mess. I always *have*. I always *will*. (*Rather defiantly.*) *You* are forcin' this trouble—you won't listen to what—

MISS MYRTLE
Don't talk about *me*. It's *her* I'm tryin' to save.

MR. FISHBACK
But you won't let me tell you—

MISS MYRTLE
No, but I don't want any more of your whining. You better dry up. I'll soon be through with you. But if you give it away, you know what I'll do.

MR. FISHBACK
Can't I say—

MISS MYRTLE
No, nothin'. I will give you the extension on the note providin' you do as I told you. You've got to give her up. We've talked it over. It's a bargain. You keep pretty mum. I'll do the talkin'.

MR. FISHBACK
You're making a mistake.

MISS MYRTLE
We'll just make her *believe* that you've changed your mind—that you and me, after all these

years, has made up. That it's *me* you want to marry, not *her*. She'll see what a rattlesnake you are.

(*Mr. Fishback, by this time, has sunk into a chair, seeing the impossiblity of reasoning with her.*)

But remember, you don't dare to give it away. If you do I'll make you a bankrupt.

MR. FISHBACK

If you'd only listen and let me tell you—

(*The door opens, silencing them. Enter Miss Pansy, stopping as if surprised.*)

MISS PANSY

Myrtle? Mr. Fishback?

MISS MYRTLE

Yes, we have come—together.

MISS PANSY

Together?

MISS MYRTLE

To see you. To talk to you. To tell you something.

(*Mr. Fishback has risen. But he does not look Pansy in the face. He has a hangdog, guilty expression. It is an awkward situation. All seem hesitant, all nervous. Pansy looks at both inquiringly.*)

MISS PANSY

To tell me something?

MISS MYRTLE

Yes, I might as well say it right out. Mr. Fishback and me has talked things over. In fact, we've made up. I've consented—that is, I—I've said "Yes" to Mr. Fishback—

(*Miss Pansy is greatly embarrassed and is in a sort of silly fluster, thinking her sister has consented to her marriage with Mr. Fishback.*)

MISS PANSY

Oh, Myrtle! (*Turning eagerly to Mr. Fishback who is looking away.*)

MISS MYRTLE

I—I—*I* am going to marry Mr. Fishback. He's asked *me.*

MISS PANSY (*dazed and reeling*)

You are going to marry Mr. Fishback? (*She looks at him appealingly.*)

MISS MYRTLE

Yes.

MISS PANSY

You and him?

MISS MYRTLE

Yes.

(*Miss Pansy, clutching a table, is about to faint. Mr. Fishback makes a move toward her, but hesitates at a warning from Miss Myrtle.*)

MISS PANSY (*gaining control*)

I thought you meant—I—you—why didn't you tell me that a while ago?

MISS MYRTLE

I didn't know it then.

MR. FISHBACK

I'm sorry—I am always making mistakes. I think . . . . .

(*Miss Myrtle silences him with a glance.*)

MISS MYRTLE

Why, Pansy, don't act so surprised. You know he and me—for all these years—I was mistaken this morning—you, I—you are younger than me—you can find someone else. (*Miss Pansy continues her appealing glances at Mr. Fishback, who drops his head and stands as a condemned man receiving his sentence.*) I didn't mean to take him away from you. (*Forlornly.*) But—well, you see this is the way it turned out.

(*Miss Pansy gains more control of herself. But she speaks as if her mind is far off, and with a crisis past, is planning what to do.*)

MISS PANSY (*first appraising Mr. Fishback completely and finding him a most miserable and disgusting specimen of manhood*)

You can have him.

MISS MYRTLE

You don't hate him?

MISS PANSY (*rather wildly*)

I am thinking of *myself*, not him, nor you.

MISS MYRTLE

You're not mad at *me?*

MISS PANSY (*slowly*)

No. I ain't mad—I don't know what to do.

MISS MYRTLE

But you talk so strange. (*Miss Myrtle begins to sniffle.*)

MR. FISHBACK

Now, Miss Myrtle—

(*Miss Myrtle now weeps, but without human fervor. Miss Pansy becomes more natural. She has still greater control now. She looks pityingly at Mr. Fishback, then goes to Miss Myrtle, takes her in her arms and kisses her, but it is mere formality. They both sob. Mr. Fishback sits, disconsolately.*)

MISS PANSY

There, there, Myrtle, don't cry. Maybe it'll turn out for the best. Somehow, I'm younger than you—I can take care of myself. You can have him. If he can repay you—Don't cry, now.

(*She motions Mr. Fishback to come over, and to his surprise she transfers Miss Myrtle to him. Awkwardly, he tries to soothe her, but Miss Myrtle releases herself, somewhat embarrassed.*)

MISS MYRTLE

You're so good, Pansy. So Christianlike.

MR. FISHBACK

Yes, you're— (*He shrivels up at the contemptuous look he sees in Pansy's face.*)

MISS PANSY

Lunch is ready out there. Why don't you invite Mr. Fishback to set down and have a bite with you?

(*She is putting on her coat and hat. From now on, Mr. Fishback becomes much more distressed and nervous. He starts to interrupt and stops. He twists his hat and shows other signs of anguish.*)

84

MISS MYRTLE
But where are *you* going?

MISS PANSY
To the hotel.

MISS MYRTLE AND MR. FISHBACK (*astonished*)
To the hotel?

MISS PANSY
Yes.

MISS MYRTLE
But why? *You* can have the store, now that I'm going to the farm to live. I thought you understood *that*.

MISS PANSY
I am going to the hotel.

MISS MYRTLE
Tell me why.

MISS PANSY
To get a job.

MISS MYRTLE AND MR. FISHBACK
A job!

MISS PANSY
Yes, waiting on table. (*Softly*.) Maybe I'll meet—a drummer.

(*Miss Myrtle and Mr. Fishback look at each other in astonishment at the turn of affairs. Miss Pansy is at the door. She opens it, starts to step out, when Mr. Fishback, losing control, suddenly dashes forward.*)

MR. FISHBACK
No, by God! She can't go. She's bluffing. I'll tell the secret. (*But he is suddenly hesitant after this explosion. He looks at Pansy, who stands*

85

now, with her head down, in his former pose of guilt.) She—I—we—

MISS MYRTLE

Speak, man!

MR. FISHBACK

Pansy, you— *(He turns imploringly to Miss Myrtle.)* Now, Miss Myrtle, please— *(He pulls out his handkerchief, wiping off the perspiration.)*

MISS MYRTLE

Don't be a booby. What's that secret?

MR. FISHBACK *(hesitatingly)*

Well—we—we *gotta* get married!

(Miss Myrtle hesitates, stunned by this terrific blow. Then she rushes at him, with clawing hands, as if to choke him, but turns violently on Pansy, who clutches droopingly at the door jamb.)

MISS MYRTLE

Pansy, is it true? *(To Mr. Fishback.)* You liar! *(Miss Pansy does not answer, but sobs, conveying that ancient confession. Miss Myrtle goes to her and puts her arms about her gently and leads her to a chair.)* Tell me, Pansy—quick!

(Miss Pansy, midst great sobbing, whispers the confirmation in her ear. Miss Myrtle backs away, aghast.)

MISS MYRTLE

Oh, my God! *You* too?

(Realizing the truth, she again rushes at Mr. Fishback, in fury. He sits in a collapsed lump,

86

his head in his hands. He does not look up at her. She acts as if she were going to tear him to pieces. But she suddenly stops, expresses futility, gains control, stands as a stony statue. He looks up. She points him to the door. He arises and goes toward it, hesitating a minute, then turns timidly to face her.)

MISS MYRTLE (*once more her usual self, speaks with her natural frigidity*)
Then get the license.

CURTAIN

NOT IN THE LESSONS

PERSONS IN THE PLAY

ETHELYN, *the Village "Vamp"*
AMANDA LUMM, *a Teacher*
FRED SNELLENBERG, *a Hesitant Beau*
MR. LEROY, *a Mysterious Stranger*

NOT IN THE LESSONS

Of course, there is a boarding house in Red Bud, as there is in every countryside village in darkest Iowa. And, of course, the sitting-room at Mrs. Smith's boarding house is not unlike thousands of others.

It is cheaply furnished—not sparsely, but in a cosy combination of Early Pullman and Late Premium. There are the usual strange and fancy chairs, and the tidies, tables, and wall-desk that become old, but never antique, before their time.

Matisse or Cézanne would have revelled in the utter disregard of clashing colors—the carpet is an arsenical green, the wall-paper is of an unfortunate shade of red—far brighter than Mrs. Smith had expected from the sample.

And the pictures! "A Yard of Pansies," "The Stag at Eve," and "The Horse Fair" mingle riotously with family groups and crayon enlargements of the departed.

There is a phonograph of the horn variety. And an upright piano. And an old-fashioned walnut pier mirror.

Altogether, it is just such a room as clutching climbers in metropolitan society who are "nearly there" often remember distastefully as their habitat of earlier years, before they came to the city and made their money—the sort of a room that such people never, never confess.

One long side wall opens out on the front porch.

It is an early evening in May and the screen door is already placed. There is a window, too, on this wall, and through it we see that Mrs. Smith has brought out the porch chairs.

Another wall reveals a door leading to the kitchen. On the opposite side of the room are two doors, one leading to the parlor bedroom, the other to the hall.

Supper is over, but the boarders have not lingered indoors.

However, there are two occupants of the room— Amanda Lumm and Mrs. Smith's daughter, Ethelyn.

Ethelyn, recently plain Ethel, is the village "vamp." She is about eighteen years old—old enough to know better. But she is an inveterate admirer of the movies, and has become infatuated with the vampire queens of the screen. She affects their snaky poses.

She is gowned in a tight, black dress—her conception of a tragedienne's costume. She has large, black earrings and a pretentious, imitation pearl necklace. Her dress is cut lower than usual in Red Bud. She wears high-heeled pumps. Her hair is marvelously coiffed, with an enormous "bun" over each ear, and the usual void at the back of her head. She is "made up" to an extreme.

Unfortunately, though, her figure is a little too plump for a slithering vampire. Unfortunately, her hair is too light. One imagines that, to be the real thing, she would need a strict and sour diet and much hair-dye. Furthermore, in moments of inactivity, her face beams a kindly, rural friendliness. Alas, it is difficult for her to make herself wicked!

She continually "acts." She strives for effects. She watches herself in the mirror, admiring her poses. She attempts constantly to approximate the seductive charms of the most noted vampires of the celluloid drama.

In contrast, Amanda Lumm, the high-school teacher boarding at Mrs. Smith's, is conservative and inconspicuous in her attire. She wears a simple tailored dress. She is about twenty-five years old. One imagines that she tones "down" while Ethelyn tones "up." Her prim restraint is more typical of Red Bud, but one is puzzled by her and inclined to speculate.

For instance, one might imagine her a far better "vamp" than Ethelyn. Her hair is jet black and there is plenty of it. She has a pallor that might be considered stagey. She is thin and might be sinuous. She has a musical, throaty voice.

But as a high-school teacher, unmarried, living at a boarding house, she has always set an example of maidenly reserve.

Amanda and Ethelyn are in the midst of a conversation. Amanda is rather bored and lays aside her book with reluctance, while Ethelyn forces upon her the latest examples of her art, as it is developing under the postal tutelage of the World-wide Photo Drama College.

ETHELYN
Next I'll give you that scene from "Visions of

Cleopatra." It's in Lesson Ten. You can just imagine the scene. (*Picking up a booklet and reading from it.*) "Cleopatra is lying on a gorgeous divan with slaves fanning her. She is alluringly gowned in greenish gauze and spangles, and laden with precious jewels." You'll have to imagine the costume, too. And how it would all look in the film. This is the way the lesson says to do it.

(*She goes over and lies down on the sofa in her interpretation of luxurious abandon. She motions to an imaginary slave, whispers in his ear, and then, in an imperious manner, directs him to depart. She then ends the scene and sits up quite naturally.*)

ETHELYN

That's just when Cleopatra sends for Anthony. You know, this is the part Theda Bara played. That's my lesson *this* week. Last week I did Sappho.

AMANDA (*stifling a yawn*)

You did Sappho?

ETHELYN

Yes. Ain't correspondence courses wonderful! I know I'm a born movie actress, and I expect to get my diploma earlier than usual. They say one should go slow. They say it should take two years to finish the course. But *I* think that is for the people who ain't got talent, who ain't as artistic as me. (*Looking inquiringly at Amanda, as if for confirmation.*)

AMANDA

Well, I don't know much about it—you see, I—

ETHELYN

Oh, I know you are simply dippy over your books. You read such queer things, too. What *do* you see in them? Now *I* like novels.

AMANDA

As I was going to say, I don't know much about acting—and I've hardly got over your ambitions to be a musician. This movie course you are taking up came so suddenly—I was just getting used to your practicing, when you gave up that zither course.

ETHELYN (*disdainfully*)

Oh, that! I should have took up the ukulele, anyhow. The zither is going out of fashion. (*Reminiscently.*) But music—I don't take to it like art. It wasn't nearly as interesting as that course in china painting.

AMANDA

Is it hard—learning to act by mail?

ETHELYN

Well, for *some* people—but *I* don't find it hard. It just seems to come to me naturally. The lessons say that some people are just natural-born actresses, and I think I—well, I just live in a trance lately. I just can't wait to finish the course! I'm just crazy to go to a studio and show the director what I can do. Just think of the big salaries! And the star's jewelry! And her limousine! Her clothes! Her maids!

(A muffled voice, that of Ethelyn's mother, is heard from the next room. The call is yodled.)

VOICE

Ethel. Ethel.

(Ethelyn opens the door to the kitchen.)

ETHELYN

Yes, Mom. What is it, Mom? *(To Amanda.)* She *will* call me Ethel instead of Ethelyn.

VOICE

Come, wipe the supper dishes.

ETHELYN

Oh, Mom, didn't you know Miss Lumm was down in the parlor?

VOICE

Well, she won't mind settin' there a bit.

ETHELYN *(pouting)*

Now, Mom—

VOICE

I bet you're jest gassin', anyways.

ETHELYN *(whining)*

But Mom—

VOICE

Well, let it go *this* time. I'll do it. But you gotta empty the—

(Ethelyn slams the door in haste, covering her ears and affecting dramatic disgust.)

ETHELYN *(looking appealingly at Amanda)*

You see how it is, Amanda. How my artistic temperment is crushed. I am held down— I can't devote enough time to my art. I tell you people will be sorry some day, when I become a famous actress, that they didn't help instead of hinder me. Now, there's Mom—she's terrible. Mothers never *understand* their daughters.

AMANDA

The new minister said last Sunday that daughters never *understood* their mothers.

ETHELYN

Fudge on him. He's an old mossback, even if he is young.

AMANDA

Mrs. Upjohn said he was interested in you. He keeps looking at you all the time.

ETHELYN (*momentarily flattered*)

He does? (*But changing her mind.*) No, he doesn't like me. He speaks against the stage. He doesn't understand me. Few people understand me. Artists are never understood, are they? But *you*, you seem to understand me more than anyone else in Red Bud. And it's funny, too. Ever since you got back from the U and began teaching, you've been so sort of strange—reading all those queer books, paying no attention to men, and going your own way. (*Picking up Amanda's book and reading the title,* "*The Woman of Tomorrow.*") What's it all about? Tell me, why is it that every girl that goes over to the State U always comes back so changed? (*The telephone rings. Ethelyn answers it.*) Hullo. Yes. This is Ethelyn. (*Pause.*) No. Who? Oh, yes, Charlie Menk. (*With more reserve.*) No, I have a date. Yes. Tonight and tomorrow night. (*Making faces at him over the telephone for Amanda's benefit.*) What? What did you say? Why *Mr.* Menk! (*Registers horror and embarrassment to Amanda.*) Oh, I see. I thought you meant it the other way. (*Pause, then sudden affability.*) Well, I might take a little, teensy-weensy ride with you tonight, if we go right away. I gotta date at eight-thirty. I gotta get back. (*Pause.*) Oh, that will be fine. Yes. Yes. Bye-bye. (*Leaves the telephone.*)

(*To Amanda.*) That was Charlie Menk. Ain't he grand? But so rough! What he learned in France was a-plenty. You oughta heard what he said to me! And I just bet them telephone operators listen in.

AMANDA

What did he say?

ETHELYN (*coquettishly*)

I can't repeat it—it was the *way* he said it. He wants me to go autoing with him. And he called it a "spoony-moon" trip. And said—oh, he's just a terrible spooner.

AMANDA

The girls say he isn't quite nice any more.

ETHELYN

That's because they ain't got temperment. A little spooning ain't gonna hurt. For *me*, it's just practice. So I encourage 'em. And I think you oughta loosen up a little, Amanda—you're so kinda distant. You'll be an old maid sure, if you ain't careful.

AMANDA

But I don't see what you mean by going out

this way with Charlie Menk, when, if you wanted to, you could get engaged to Fred Snellenberger. And he's the one, isn't he, who's coming this evening?

ETHELYN

Yes, it's him. And he'll be *so* jealous. If he comes while I'm gone, you talk to him, won't you? You and him went to the U at the same time, and he's sorta fond of books. Maybe you could keep him interested talking about the latest novels. He ain't hard to entertain—he's so shy. (*Kittenishly, and as though she considered it a great joke.*) But don't vamp him, Amanda, now—will you?

AMANDA (*amused but professing surprise*)

Why, Ethelyn! I vamp Fred? How can you be so silly?

ETHELYN

Well, I may want him and I may not. But I want to keep him guessing. With my career ahead of me I may not want to marry soon. In Lesson Four it says, "No great actress can afford to be tied down by conventions."

AMANDA

Those lessons sound terrible. I'd never want to be an actress. I'm afraid I'm too conventional.

ETHELYN

Do *you* know of a great actress tied down? They divorce their husbands. Why, before I'm through, I may have a half-dozen husbands. They all do.

AMANDA

That's scandalous.

99

ETHELYN (*dramatically*)
A soul like mine is above the sordid things. I yearn for the mountain tops of success, with millions at my feet worshipping the very ground I walk on.

(*The muffled and yodling voice of her mother is heard in the next room.*)

VOICE
Ethel. Ethel.

(*Ethelyn opens the door in disgust.*)

ETHELYN
Yes, Mom. What is it now?

VOICE
Come and empty the slop out to the chickens.

ETHELYN (*in a petulant rage*)
Oh, fudge! Excuse me, Amanda, I'll go out and get it over with. (*She flounces out.*)

(*Enter Mr. Leroy from his parlor bedroom. He is a tony dresser, in grey and white checked suit, loud vest, etc. He carries a pearl-grey derby. His manner, however, is dour and funereal.*)

MR. LEROY
Good evening, Miss Lumm.

AMANDA
Good evening, Mr. Leroy.

(*He looks at the mail on the table, sorts it, picks out a letter and opens it. Reads it. Puts it in his pocket.*)

AMANDA

Ahem! Ahem! Do you like Red Bud, Mr. Leroy?

MR. LEROY (*who is about to explode with laughter at this question*)

Like it! (*But he catches himself in time and reverts to his funereal attitude.*) Yes, I like it.

AMANDA

After Chicago?

MR. LEROY

Well—you see—Chicago—I—Miss Lumm, there is something I want to say to you— (*Enter Ethelyn, to his disgust.*) Good evening, Miss Smith.

ETHELYN (*beaming and vampirish*)

Same to you, Mr. Leroy. Won't you set down? We like to have the boarders use the parlor when they feel lonesome.

MR. LEROY (*sliding away towards the entrance door*)

Thank you, Miss Smith, not now. I was just going for a walk. (*He opens the door and leaves hastily.*)

ETHELYN

Ain't he queer?

AMANDA

Who is this Mr. Leroy?

ETHELYN

Mom don't know. Once in a while we have a stray boarder like him, who don't stay at the hotel. He paid for a week in advance. This is his fourth day.

AMANDA

Is he going to be here long?

ETHELYN

Don't know. But ain't he a swell dresser?
(*The honk-honk of an automobile is heard.*) That's
Charlie. (*Putting on her hat.*) You keep Fred
waiting for me. I'll be right back, sure. (*She
goes out.*)

(*Miss Lumm takes up her book and reads, but
looks up as if her mind was not quite settled
on its contents. She lays it aside for a moment,
goes and appraises herself in the mirror. Then
goes back, sits down, is contemplative for a moment, shrugs her shoulders, and indicates throwing off the subject that she is thinking about. She
picks up the book and reads again, settling down
cosily for a comfortable session.
But hardly has she read a bit, when Fred Snellenberger comes to the door, looks in, knocks. Miss
Lumm calls "Come in." He enters. He is a
husky young fellow, about twenty-five, athletically
set up. His suit and collar are somewhat tight
as though he had found his "civvies" a trifle small.*)

FRED

Hello, Amanda.

AMANDA

Hello, Fred.

FRED

Is Ethelyn here?

AMANDA

She will be here in a little while. She said for
you to make yourself at home. And for us to
talk together until she came.

FRED

Where is she?

AMANDA

Oh, she'll be back shortly.

FRED

It's a wonderful spring evening, isn't it?

AMANDA

Yes; isn't it lovely!

FRED

Sort of reminds me of those days over at the U, particularly the two of us sitting together—and you always with your books. (*He examines one of her books, noting the title, "The Riddle of the Universe."*) Haeckel, eh? You still keep up, don't you?

AMANDA

Yes, and you should, too, Fred. Surely going into your father's store hasn't ended everything for you, has it?

FRED

Well, the War—oh, I've never been the same since I got back. I think everything seems to be hopeless. I'm sort of a fatalist now, you know.

AMANDA

But do you try to—why, Fred, you were one of the smartest men in our class.

FRED

Yes, I know, but things are far different now. I just live from day to day. I don't plan like I used to.

AMANDA

Seems to me you have been planning *one* thing, at least.

FRED

What?

AMANDA

Getting married. You *are* determined, aren't you?

FRED (*flushing and surprised*)

Why, Amanda!

AMANDA

Well, now, let's talk like we used to. That *is* what's the matter with you lately, isn't it? Rushing one girl after another. It couldn't be anything else. Do you mind talking frankly like we did at the U?

FRED

I don't know how to take you, Amanda.

AMANDA

It'll come back to you. And somebody must set you right. I've watched you right along, since you got back home, and I know just how you feel—this May madness—it makes one desperate.

FRED

Now, Amanda, I never did any girl any harm, and you know it.

AMANDA

Oh, I'm not saying you have—not at all. I wasn't thinking of that. Probably you haven't. But I figure you are suffering from suppressed desire.

FRED

From what?

AMANDA

Not that I mind it in the least. It is perfectly natural, perfectly normal. Girls have it, too.

FRED

Well, I'm not ailing. I came back from France altogether shipshape.

AMANDA

It isn't that you're sick like we know it around here. Nor like shell-shock and things men got in the war. It's something else—this May madness.

FRED

Something out of your books?

AMANDA

Why don't you cure yourself at once? Why don't you pick out the girl and get her.

FRED

You've never talked to me like this before, Amanda. You talk so different than when we were at the U.

AMANDA

I say, marry her!

FRED

Her? What her?

AMANDA

Any her.

FRED

But maybe she won't have me. Maybe she isn't the right one.

AMANDA

Afraid? And you with the Croix de Guerre?

FRED

Well, you know how it is—

AMANDA

You can make any girl have you. And make-any one the right one. Don't you understand? A woman still wants a man to steal her.

FRED

You mean to elope?

AMANDA

Oh, not that exactly. But elope, if you want to. I mean, you men wait and wait always until a woman grabs *you*. When all the time she wants you to take her. Or to feel that you have, even if she has pulled the strings a tiny bit.

FRED

But I'm not romantic like the heroes in those books.

AMANDA

I don't read hero books.

FRED

Well, then, those psychology books you've been reading ever since I can remember.

AMANDA

What I'm trying to get you into thinking about is not romance, but just an ordinary fact. A fact that every woman—well, it's instinct with her—while you men make it so complex.

FRED

So you think marrying a girl is pretty ordinary?

AMANDA

Yes, and you will, too, a while after you're married. Not that I want to destroy all your illusions.

FRED

Illusions?

AMANDA

Yes, all the fuss and feathers about finding your *right* mate. That's poppycock. Tommyrot. It's a physical thing, a mental thing, not a soul thing. This soul-mate drivel—don't you see that love is not so much what it is, as what you make it?

FRED

What about marriages being made in heaven?

AMANDA (*laughing*)

The idea of heaven being connected with you and Ethelyn is—well, I'm afraid I've shocked you enough. Come, do you want Ethelyn?

FRED

Well, I can't say. I'm not decided. I—

AMANDA

You've got her on a sort of trial?

FRED

Well, this play-acting—now, what do you think about it? Do you think she will go into the movies?

AMANDA

Do you ask that seriously?

FRED

Yes—seriously.

AMANDA

That is a joke. I don't say it to hurt your feelings, but to help you—when you are so juvenile. She will never leave Red Bud, probably. She will never go on the stage. Can't you see that her life is—as a wife?

107

FRED

But what about her artistic career—she's always talking about it.

AMANDA

Her most artistic career will be having about a half-dozen babies.

FRED

Why, Amanda!

AMANDA

Oh, I might just as well talk it out with you— you poor, benighted boy. Can't you see? Can't you understand her sudden desire to become an actress? Don't you remember her spell when she was going to become a great musician? Before that it was painting. Before that—well, that was before I came here to board. She has one craze after another. One spasm of effort after another. *She's* suffering from the same thing *you're* suffering.

FRED

But I'm not—

AMANDA

Oh, yes you are. You've made up you're mind that you must get married, now haven't you? You're on pins and needles until you do. You can't resist it. You just must. That's the way with her. What she wants is to be captured. But with all you men just rushing her and nothing else—none of you marrying her—she's got to blow off steam some other way. She doesn't take all your parlor-petting seriously. What she needs is a baby instead of lessons in acting.

RED

But why pick on *me*?

AMANDA

Well, do you know anybody else you'd rather have as the mother of your children?

FRED

Of course I like her. I am very fond of her. But I can't decide whether she'd settle down. And in the meantime—

AMANDA

You could settle her pretty quick. And she'd be the most natural sort of a meek little mother in a year or two that you ever saw.

FRED

You think I could do anything with any woman?

AMANDA

Oh, don't flatter yourself so. The woman usually arranges it. It's a woman's natural instinct to parade domesticity before her little world.

FRED

But *you*? And all those suffragettes? All those advanced thinkers?

AMANDA

They're just the few unsexed. Or oversexed.

FRED

And *you*?

AMANDA (*slightly disconcerted at his manner*)

We're talking about *you* and Ethelyn.

FRED

But I've been liking *you* all this time, too. But you're always big-sistering me.

AMANDA

Now don't start anything like that. You're just temporarily overcome by what you think is a flow of logic. Don't be misled. You're not looking for logic. What you're looking for is something else. And you won't be happy until you have it.

(*Mr. Leroy appears at the porch window—visible to the audience, but not to Amanda and Fred.*)

FRED

Why, we've known each other all these years—through school— through the U—then since. Do you think you might like me enough to —some day—

AMANDA

You *are* getting silly. I don't want you to practice on *me*. I want you to practice on Ethelyn. Rush her off her feet. Marry her at once. Wind her around your little finger. Give her a lot of children. Submerge her. Pet her. Stunt her. Dominate her. And she'll love you till your dying day.

(*She turns away from him, going over to sit down on the sofa. He stands behind her. He throws his shoulders back and stands at attention in a military manner for a moment. Then he transforms into the primitive hunter, sneaks stealthily upon her, and before she knows it, he is beside her, clasping her to him in frenzied embrace, covering her with kisses. She strives to release her-*)

self, even fights. But his strength is too much. There is a fury in his abandon and a wildness in his conquering affections. Finally she pushes him aside, as they leap up, facing each other in battle.)

AMANDA (*flushing and righting her hair*)
What madness!

FRED
Something came over me—

AMANDA
May madness!

FRED
I just couldn't help it—I did what you said—you know now—

AMANDA
You scared me.

FRED
I love you.

AMANDA
No, you don't. You love *love*.

FRED
I love *you*.

AMANDA
Oh, you're hopeless. Utterly mistaken. The idea—here in this room—with Ethelyn due any minute. And some of the other boarders might have come in.

FRED
Will you marry me? Will you elope with me to Chicago? Tonight? (*Pleading*) Don't you like the idea? Just a little—just enough?

AMANDA

No; it's a crazy idea. Take my advice and marry Ethelyn—*quick!* For your own sake. I am going to my room—you've mussed me all up.

FRED (*forlornly*)

I don't want to see Ethelyn, *now.*

AMANDA

Now? What do you mean? You don't think that I have taken you seriously? Sit down and cool off. Then try it on Ethelyn. She'll like it. You did very well. Really—very well.

(*But Fred suddenly clasps her again, holding her taut. She struggles—not so wildly as before. There is a faint hint of acquiescence and response. Mr. Leroy is seen at the door. He coughs warningly, then enters. They hear him. Fred releases Amanda quickly, as they stand, embarrassed.*)

MR. LEROY

Great! (*He claps his hands.*) What a wonderful fade-out!

FRED (*belligerently*)

What do you mean? It's none of your business. Say another word and I'll knock your block off, you Peeping Tom.

MR. LEROY (*suavely*)

Now keep your hat on! No harm's meant. (*He goes over to Amanda and addresses her in his brisk, brusque manner, holding out a paper and fountain pen.*) Yes, $100 a week for you. Sign here. A new movie actress discovered. A new queen of Hollywood.

AMANDA

What are you talking about? I never heard such chatter. (*To Fred.*) Is he insane, or are we?

FRED

Yes, explain yourself, or get out.

MR. LEROY

Simple. I offer Miss Lumm $100 a week. As a movie actress she'll shoot better than Theda. I am a character scout for the Inter-Constellation Photo Play Corporation. I tour the country looking for talent. Miss Lumm has been under my observation for four days. She is a born knock-out—or, as the director would say: "beautiful, graceful, emotional, correct facial expressions, eyes that register well, the right complexion, wonderful hair." With a little training—a very little—she will shove 'em all off the pedestal. She'll make Mary Pickford and Theda Bara and Olga Petrova and all of 'em sit up and take notice. Why, the country'll go mad over her.

AMANDA (*dazed*)

Fifty dollars a *month* now. Why, one hundred dollars a *week* sounds like a dream.

FRED

Sounds like a fake to me.

MR. LEROY

I blew in here looking for characters for a new series of rural farces—boob stuff. I was directed to Red Bud by a friend, the manager of a movie-acting correspondence school. He said the young lady living here, Miss Smith, is a pupil.

Her lessons and correspondence were such a scream that my pal says to me: "Scoot out there and give her the once over—she might be a comedian and not know it." (*To Amanda.*) But *you*, you're some tragedy queen!

AMANDA

Ethelyn—a scream—a comedian?

FRED (*to Mr. Leroy*)

Don't be insulting.

MR. LEROY (*to Fred*)

And you, young man, I ain't got your name, but we can certainly find a place for you—as a lover, you're a bear—take it from me. All the dames ought to be crazy about you. You make a regular he-man idol, I'll tell the world.

FRED

That's damed nonsense. (*To Amanda.*) Sounds bug-house to me.

MR. LEROY

Say, I want you to shoot that clutch over again. I didn't get the beginning very well. It was all so sudden.

AMANDA

Mr. Leroy! Don't you understand? We're not amateur actors. It's *Miss Smith* that's interested in the movies.

MR. LEROY (*surprised*)

Oh, it was *real* then. (*Confidentially.*) Well, I gotta hand it to you. I thought it was pretty natural. And you can act in the movies *together*, when you're married. (*He smirks.*)

AMANDA

Married? We have no such intention.

MR. LEROY (*with an intimate smile*)
All right—if that is the way you feel about it.
I understand. I thought—but we never in-
quire into the personal relationships of our
casts. If there is a reason for this soul stuff—
we just wink.

FRED (*again belligerent*)
Say, you'd better be careful with your tongue.
If you make any more insinuations, I'll put you
out.

MR. LEROY (*soothingly*)
My friend, let's get down to the dotted line. I
make you people this offer—

AMANDA
I'd never consider it. You've made a mistake.
(*To Fred.*) Oh, Fred, it seems like I'm drowning
—grasping at straws—tell me I'm not dreaming
—save me—send him away.

MR. LEROY
Oh, cheese the sob-stuff and think of your career!
Think of the fortune you'd make. Think of the
millions who'd admire you. Think of leaving
this jay burg. Think of everybody turning to
look at you on the street. Why, you'd make a
famous vamp.

AMANDA
Vamp? I? Why, I'm not the type. Ethelyn—

MR. LEROY
If you mention her name again, I'll go nuts.
There's a million—a billion—a trillion, like her.
But *you*— you are one of the few, the rare birds.
Now, think it over, this proposition. You at
one hundred dollars a week, your gentleman

friend here at—well, we'll take care of him. He can be with you. (*With a meaning smile.*)
I'm going to my room to write headquarters that I've discovered a new darling of the screen.

AMANDA

Do nothing of the sort. You see (*looking shyly at Fred*) I might have other interests—more alluring.

FRED (*to Mr. Leroy*)

Yes, hold your horses. You're in too much of a hurry.

MR. LEROY

Oh, I'm sure you'll agree. Think it over. Think it over. (*He goes to his room, turning at the door to address them.*) But for goodness' sakes, don't tell that—that student who I am.

(*They sit down, both flabbergasted, overcome by all the recent happenings. A momentary pause.*)

AMANDA

Ethelyn—will—be here—soon. I'm going.

FRED

Please don't go.

AMANDA

I cannot stay.

FRED

If you must leave me, think about my idea. Tonight. Chicago. I'm going—you come with me—I mean it. I meant everything. It's *you*—

AMANDA

Fred—you owe it to Ethelyn. She—

(In dashes Ethelyn, impersonating her idea of a tragedy role.)

ETHELYN

So here you are. I've caught you, haven't I? (*She comes over to them.*) I just met Mrs. Upjohn, who had been here to call and stood right there on the porch and was so shocked she didn't knock. She said "Don't go in there and interrupt them turtle-doves."
So, Amanda, you are trying to steal him, are you? Trying to rob me of him? Right here in my own home. Trying to vamp him, eh, while I'm away. And I thought you were my friend! Oh, what can a woman do when another sets out to steal her man!

AMANDA

Why, Ethelyn—I—

ETHELYN

Don't—don't deny. I know it is true. I know. I'm psychic. You have tried to win him away from me.

FRED

Nothing of the sort. I was the—

ETHELYN (*to Fred*)

Of course, men are *never* to blame. I know you never turned your hand, Fred. It is the woman who pursues. Only I didn't pursue hard enough. I know you weren't the one to blame, for I know how hard it is for you to spoon. Now, Charlie Menk, he is—

AMANDA

You must stop this. I won't stand for it. I never—oh, it is all so ridiculous. I—

ETHELYN

Don't deny. I know I am a real psychic. I just felt this would happen. And I am going to take up a course in spiritualism. I know I could be a medium. I must write for catalogues tomorrow of the spiritualistic schools. I know I can learn it by mail.

AMANDA (*disgusted and about to leave the room by door at front right*) Tell her, Fred, if you can get her to listen. (*To Ethelyn.*) Fred wants to have a talk with you.

FRED (*rushing over to Amanda as she leaves*) Think over that idea, Amanda, won't you?

(*Amanda leaves as Fred looks at her appealingly, unseen by Ethelyn.*)

ETHELYN

Well?

FRED (*in a rather contemplative mood*) I wonder—I wonder if you *do* care for me? If we really are engaged? I can't tell. I want to know. Now. You've said a lot of things— did you mean them? You wrote such letters when I was in the army—and everything. And when I got back—I wonder—I wonder what's to prove whether we're engaged. (*With a sudden inspiration.*) Mrs. Upjohn fibbed!

ETHELYN (*surprised*) That makes no difference. Where's smoke, there's flame. I guess you were both embarrassed enough to give it away.

FRED (*lying glibly*)

Merely at the way you were acting. I tell you there's nothing to it. You're mistaken. Let's make up.

ETHELYN

Do you really—well, you've proposed so many times. But without that divine—divine—oh, I forget what Lesson Six says. Now, Charlie Menk, he—you are always so cold.

FRED

You think so?

ETHELYN

Anyhow, I'm going into the movies.

(*She is sitting on the sofa and Fred moves behind a distance and the scene duplicates that between him and Amanda. He appraises Ethelyn questioningly for a moment, then shows decision. He lunges forward and captures her in his arms and covers her with impassioned kisses. It is identically the way he treated Amanda. But Ethelyn takes it all calmly, making no protests, no struggles. She takes it for granted. So it ends with Fred's dropping her on the sofa, releasing himself, and standing off as she calmly rights her hair.*
He is disgusted and shows it plainly, unconsciously wiping off his coat sleeves. It was a failure. The disillusionment is complete. He backs away, thoroughly uncomfortable.)

119

ETHELYN

You're improving. A little more practice and I might accept a ring. But it was pretty crude. Now *I* like refinement. Charlie Menk is so— well, *you're* not of an emotional temperment.

FRED

You thought I was practicing?

ETHELYN

Well, what's a beau for?

FRED

You know how long we've been sort of engaged —long before I went into the army. That is, if you think we *are* engaged. I'm commencing to have my doubts. I must know—tonight.

ETHELYN

Tonight? What's the hurry?

FRED

Why can't we cut out all this guff and get married right away. (*He looks at her anxiously.*)

ETHELYN

But my career!

(*He is relieved.*)

FRED

Oh, damn, I mean, durn your career. What you need is a husband, and a—a b-baby.

ETHELYN (*in a tragedy pose as if he had struck her*)

Why, Fred. A baby! Don't you think it! I got my career to consider.

FRED

You've said you loved me. You wrote those let-ters. And I don't want to wait and keep on waiting. "Love isn't so much what it is, as what you make it." (*He goes over to her and faces her in a final test. Tensely.*) Would you elope with me tonight?

(*As she turns away flippantly, he shows delight— the test is ended, he knows that he has won his freedom from the superficial but conventional tie between them. He relaxes.*)

ETHELYN
Why, Fred, that's really dramatic!

FRED (*slowly*)
Well, I guess we're through. I see you take nothing seriously. This has been our test. You don't want me. It's all been a mistake, (*reminiscently*) all May madness, this engagement of ours. I'm sorry. I know now I never could be happy with you. Nor you with me. We had to find out—and it's better now than later. We're misfits.

(*Mr. Leroy's door opens softly. He sticks his head out inquiringly, but withdraws quickly, leaving the door ajar. He is eavesdropping.*)

ETHELYN (*undramatically, as any village girl might act in such a crisis*)
Don't you dare talk to me that way. Just after trying to—to—vamp me.

FRED (*laughing kindly*)
Why, my dear child, I'd as soon try to win a hitching-post. There *was* a time when I thought I wanted you to marry me. I thought you'd get over those wild ideas. Now I wouldn't try

to "vamp you," as you say, if this were the
Garden of Eden.

ETHELYN (*whining*)

I'm going to call Mom.

FRED

Call her. I'm going. Then, when she comes,
give her a dose of your Camille.

(*He puts on his hat and goes toward the door,
turning to address her further, as she drops limply
into a chair, acting the part of a deserted and for-
lorn woman. Her position is well in front of
the stage. She is facing the audience, so that the
subsequent action takes place behind her.*

*Amanda, at this moment—with Fred seeing her,
but not Ethelyn—slips out of the hall into the
parlor, gowned and hatted in a travelling costume
and carrying a small bag. She comes across to
Fred, ignoring Ethelyn, who continues to sit
in a stolid pose, somewhat concealed in her big
chair. Fred looks eagerly at Amanda, holding
out his arms to her. She comes to him, smiling.*)

AMANDA (*demurely*)

I rather like *your* idea, Fred. Much *more* than
Mr. Leroy's. What time does the train leave?
(*Ethelyn starts at the voice, but does not turn
around.*) You're sure you meant it—all?

(*He kisses her softly and reverentially.*)

FRED

I've felt it all along. *But I know now!*

AMANDA (*playfully*)

But you're so timid! All of a sudden.

(*He gives her a real hug, then they depart, quickly. Ethelyn, who sits with a stupid stare, seems afraid to look around. At this moment, and unheard by Ethelyn, Mr. Leroy, dressed for departure, and carrying his suitcase, tip-toes stealthily out of his room, drops a check on the table, opens the door and rushes out to follow the elopers.*)

ETHELYN (*slowly "coming to" and attempting a piteous wail that turns out to be a real burlesque.*) But this was—*not in the lessons!* (*She looks around the room for the first time and at the door. Her daze is completely ended by a familiar yodle.*)

VOICE
Ethel—Ethel—Ethel.

ETHELYN
Yes, Mom.

VOICE
Have you set the breakfast dishes?

CURTAIN

123